ON GENDER IDENTITY

Metropolitan Youssef

ST MARY & MOSES ABBEY PRESS

On Gender Identity
By Metropolitan Youssef

Designed & Published by:
St. Mary & St. Moses Abbey Press
101 S Vista Dr, Sandia, TX 78383
stmabbeypress.com

Contents

1

God's Design for Sexuality

These are four articles on the issue of gender identity and sexuality in general, that will help us in our families, in our ministry, in the Church, and also as family servants.

To understand the issue of gender identity, and especially transgenderism, we need to understand the Biblical design for sexuality as it was instituted by God, as part of His order for creation. For without understanding God's design for sexuality, we cannot understand how to help the transgender or homosexual person, because transgenderism and homosexuality are literally changing into chaos the order that God created. And when we speak about the Biblical design for sexuality, there are three important theological principles. These principles will help us understand God's design for sexuality. The three principles are the following: 1. God created human beings as male and female; 2. God created males and females as complementary in nature; 3. God designed marriage as the context for sexual expression.

1. God Created Humans as Male and Female

At the first mention of humanity in the Scripture, we find an affirmation of the first theological principle. In Genesis, the Scripture says:

> Then God said, "Let Us make man in Our image, according to Our likeness; let them have dominion over the fish of the sea, over the birds of the air, and over the cattle, over all the earth and over every creeping thing that creeps on the earth." So God created man in His own image; in the image of God He created him; male and female He created them.[1]

These words in the first chapter of Genesis make the claim very clear. There are only two genders, male and female. But we are living in a time when distinctions between males and females are blurred, and they reject the testimony of Scripture and the order of God, in that He created only two genders. Nowadays, when people read this verse, they try to explain it, saying that this verse refers explicitly and only to the biological sex, not to gender. And they want to differentiate between sex and gender. When

---

1   Genesis 1:26–27.

they use the word biological sex, they mean the genetic and anatomical distinction that identifies the person as male and female, like the genitalia and the chromosomes, for males, XY, and for females, XX, and other biological factors that determine the maleness and femaleness in the biological sex. While we do not deny the existence of the intersex condition, it is not medically and scientifically a third biological sex. But the intersex condition speaks to us about the impact of sin on the created order that God established, to the extent that these anomalies exist and disorder God's original design. These cases are not many but rather are few. If we find a child and his chromosomes are XXY, this does not mean that there is a third biological sex, but rather it is the impact of sin on the order that God designed for sexuality.

Now, however, they define gender as the psychological and cultural component of maleness and femaleness. A distinction in gender may refer to attire, so they say, "If I feel I am a female, I will dress like a female." So is the case with activities, relationships, preferences, and even parenting styles. And different cultures may attribute certain expressions as normal for particular genders. So what is normal for a particular gender can be different from one culture to another. But historically, until approximately 50 years ago, most cultures, if not all, linked the gender norms to the biological sex. This distinction is recent, within the last 50 years. That is why the terms biological sex and gender are used synonymously in casual conversations.

But unfortunately, nowadays, the safe perception of gender is what we call gender identity; that is, how I perceive myself. Am I perceiving myself as a male or female, regardless of my biological sex? I am not saying this is correct, but I am saying that this is what they are trying to market in our contemporary time. The principle now is that gender is different from sex and that gender depends mainly on my self-perception, but sex refers to the anatomical and biological facts. They try to justify the distinction between their biological sex and gender, and use this differentiation in the transgender debate.

And the reason for this is that there was a shift in the authority. What do I mean by a shift in authority? Who decides whether you are a male or female? Until recent times, this was decided by the Word of God. God decided that there are two genders, male and female, and people believed in God. Then people started to deny God. A shift happened, and they trusted science. Because science and medicine say that there are two biological sexes, they started to believe that there are two biological sexes and associated gender with sex. Then another shift happened, and they turned to using reason and logic. And logic says if you have male genitalia and your chromosomes are XY, then you are a male. So the shift: God is the authority, science is the authority, reason is the authority.

Now, the authority is neither God nor science nor reason. But now, there is divinization of the self. I am the final authority. Self-perception became the final authority. And because of self-perception, if I feel I am a female, then I am a female. If I feel I am a male, then I am a male. And this, right now, became the final authority. And unfortunately, they try to pressure reason and science to accept this. And some people changed or altered science, medicine, and reason, trying to justify it in order to accept this.

And we hear every now and then about medical research or scientific papers that support their claim. But thanks be to God, one of the outcomes of COVID is that people no longer blindly trust scientific and medical research. Before COVID, if I said to somebody, there is research saying so and so, nobody would even try to debate it.

After COVID, however, we know as a fact that many research studies were twisted in order to justify things or explain things, leading many people to no longer trust medical research blindly. And they started to doubt their credibility, even if the research came from well-known colleges or universities. That is to say, some people in their argument will tell you, "No, there is medical research that says that gender is different from biological sex," and they will tell you, "They found something in the brain, and this is what determines the gender, not the biological sex." But we need to be careful in believing and accepting all these medical and scientific research studies, because some of them submit to the pressure from politics and the LGBTQ movement.

So now, the final authority in people's minds is self-perception, and self-perception is trying to twist reason and science, and now they are also trying to twist the Bible. And unfortunately, many churches and denominations started to provide a new theology to justify transgenderism and homosexuality, and things related to gender identity. That is why I said that the first theological principle related to the transgender debate is that God created humans as male and female. This assertion that focuses our attention on only two categories, male and female, is embedded in the order of creation for humans. God, in His economy and wisdom, created us as male and female, for a certain purpose, a certain goal. If we deny this simple reality, the fact that God created us as only male and female, then this will serve as a foundation for the transgender movement.

And now, your body is telling you something, and your mind or your feelings or your intuition is telling you something else. Your body is telling you that you are a male, but your mind is telling you that you are a female. What is the right thing to do? To align your body to your mind, or to align your mind to your body? The transgender movement wants to align their body to their mind. But is this possible? It is impossible. It is impossible medically and scientifically to convert a male to a female or a female to a male. Yes, they can give them some hormones; they can perform some surgeries, but in the end, this is just something external.

I was talking with a transgender person. He was a male, and now he is a female. And I told him that the physician who did this surgery on him and those who gave him these hormones actually committed a crime. They destroyed his body, and his body is now neither male nor female. And this is a criminal act, and they should be held accountable for these crimes that they are committing. And I asked him clearly, "What are your chromosomes?" He told me, "XY." So I told him, "Do you have a uterus? Do you have ovaries? Can you produce ova? Can you become pregnant?" And the answer was, "No; no; no; no." And I told him, "Then you are not a female."

And I told him something else: "I will give you this example, but do not take it as if I am making fun of you, because I am not. I just want you to understand. Imagine that there was a microwave, and a person decided to change this microwave into a TV. He made some changes to the microwave, so it looks like a TV. But at the end, can you watch channels on this TV that was converted from a microwave, or can you broadcast anything on it? No. So in reality, it is not a TV. Can we call it a microwave? Now, it cannot function as a microwave. So this device is now neither a microwave nor a TV. And that is exactly what has happened to your body. So even if they do not trust God or do not believe in God, it is more logical to align the mind to the body rather than to align the body to the mind."

The transgender movement wants to align the body to the mind, and this is a crime. So even those who repent and want to come back, those who want to convert back to being male, for example, their bodies are already destroyed. Maybe we can help their psychology, how to again perceive themselves as male. But the permanent damage that happened to their body cannot be changed. And this is very serious; it is a permanent destruction of the human body that cannot be reversed. That is why I pray that the government and the politicians consider these surgeries a crime and hold the physicians or the surgeons accountable for destroying the human body.

To destroy the human body that God created, you will find a lot of support; but to correct—partially correct—after this damage is done, there is no support. This is a satanic plan. To change from one sex to another is to deny biological facts and to assert something about oneself that is not observable in the physical world, even among animals. This principle is very important in the transgender debate.

I would like to give an example of a person I am dealing with. About twenty years ago, he did the surgeries and took the hormones and was married. He was a male and became a female, and was married to a male. He remained in this marriage for fifteen years. But now he realized that he had been deceived. He is not Coptic by birth but is a convert. He began to attend the Coptic Orthodox Church and learned about Orthodoxy. He wanted to repent, and the Church helped him. He repented and was baptized in the Church. We have been offering him Christian counseling. And thanks be to God that he is now in acceptance and at peace with himself, although the permanent damage done in his body cannot be changed.

He told me that twenty years ago, when he decided to do the surgeries to be a female, many companies and organizations gave him money, helped him, and supported him, and he did not pay anything. Now, however, when he tried to do some surgeries, which would only bring him back partially, the insurance companies told him that these surgeries are cosmetic and are not covered by the insurance. Surgeons are afraid or concerned about doing these surgeries, afraid of the LGBTQ movement. Neither could he find any organization to pay for these very expensive surgeries.

2. God Created Males and Females as Complementary in Nature

The second theological principle guiding our discussion is the idea that God created males and females to be complementary in nature. This, expressed through the binary sexes, falls into two categories: sexual complementarity and role complementarity. So when I say they complement each other, they complement each other in two aspects: in the sex and also in the role.

It is clear from Genesis: "Then God blessed them, and God said to them, 'Be fruitful and multiply; fill the earth and subdue it; have dominion over the fish of the sea, over the birds of the air, and over every living thing that moves on the earth.'"[2] With this pronouncement from God, we rightly know that the process through which mankind will be fruitful and multiply is the sexual relationship that God designed to take place between a man and a woman. So, when the Lord told them, "Be fruitful and multiply," how would this happen? Through the sexual relationship between them. When God created the body of the man and the body of the woman, He created them in a way that when they connect together or marry, they can reproduce. They can be fruitful and multiply.

Also, this complementarity is related to roles. So God has designed men and women to express different roles as part of their biological and psychological makeup. When God created man and woman, not only can they in their anatomy marry and have children and multiply and be fruitful, but the roles, the way men are created and women are created, are different or distinguished, but are complementary to each other. We cannot just say that men and women are different. But they are different in corresponding ways. I mean, these differences complement one another. So we can say they are complementary opposites. Yes, they are alike in their humanity but are different in the way that makes them partners. Each sex completes what the other is lacking and helps to bring the other into balance. The question is, how does the complementary nature of humans affect the transgender discussion? Because

---

2   Genesis 1:28.

sexual union is only expressed through biological distinction, it is impossible for two biological males or two biological females to be fruitful and multiply without the contribution of the other gender's gametes.

There is a man in Florida who is not Coptic. He did many surgeries to change his gender to female. I am sure you know these surgeries are artificial, and the percentage of success is very low. So after he did many surgeries to have a sexual relationship with his partner who was a male, all these surgeries failed and it was very painful, physically and psychologically, and he ended up committing suicide, because he found that all these surgeries did not help him to be a female and to have a sexual relationship with a partner, and it also caused physical pain and severe psychological pain. So he ended up committing suicide. That is why I am saying these surgeries are a crime.

When a transgender individual attempts to participate in a sexual union for the purpose of procreation, they must do it with someone of the opposite biological sex, no matter how they identify themselves. For example, if a female converts to a male, but she wants to have children, she cannot have children if she is married to another female. Because she is originally a female. If she is married to another female, they will never have children. And if she wants to have children biologically, not through adoption, the only way is to have a sexual relationship with a male, although she is claiming to be a male herself. It involves a lot of deception and lying to themselves.

Also, the role complementarity is tied to the biological and social differences between the sexes. If I am identifying myself as the opposite sex, this does not change the role complementarity that God has created. Transgenderism assumes that one can alter the gender and not minimize God's design for complementarity, but this is a false assumption.

3. God Designed Marriage as the Context for Sexual Expression

The third principle is that God designed marriage as the context for sexual expression. While this particular principle does not have direct implications in the transgender debate, it is very important because we cannot understand Biblical sexuality without this principle. We read about marriage, that when God said to them, "Be fruitful and multiply,"[3] He said, "It is not good that man should be alone; I will make him a helper comparable to him."[4] God created the woman out of man's rib, and then He presented her to him.[5] When Adam saw his wife Eve, he said "This is now bone of my bones and flesh of my flesh."[6] And there was a comment in the Scripture: "Therefore a man shall leave his father and mother and be joined to his wife, and they shall become one flesh."[7] We recognize

---

3   Genesis 1:22.
4   Genesis 2:18.
5   See Genesis 2:21–22.
6   Genesis 2:23.
7   Genesis 2:24.

that God has given marriage to humanity for the very specific purpose that includes companionship, marital union, sexual expression, procreation, faithfulness, and fidelity.

So marriage is designed by God to be a comprehensive covenant, a union between one man and one woman, intended to endure for a lifetime and closely directed toward rearing children, the next generation. Since the Biblical definition of marriage demands one man and one woman and implies that these partners will have sexual complementarity through their biological distinction, then marriage promotes an understanding of Biblical sexuality, that God created male and female, and both of them complement each other.

So, affirming the Biblical marriage means to uphold the biological distinction between men and women and the complementary nature of both their biological and psychological makings. But transgenderism promotes a disordering of marriage. For example, if a male became female, and he is married to another male, in reality, this is same-sex marriage, because a male is marrying another male.

As for the transgender people, they assume there is no necessary distinction between men and women. If a man who identifies as a woman attempts to marry from the opposite gender, this relationship cannot fulfill the sexual complementarity found in marriage, because, in the end, they are of the same sex.

17

Transgenderism also denies the long-held gender distinction when it comes to childbearing, by now promoting the idea that a man can give birth. And they are trying now to implant a uterus in males. But all these things cannot succeed.

From these three theological principles, we can see how the Scripture sets parameters around what we can accept as an appropriate expression of Biblical sexuality. But transgenderism distorts these guidelines and goes beyond the God-given design for gender expression. They cannot affirm the Biblical teaching on sexuality. That is why, when you think about transgenderism, it is not enough to say that it is an illness, but we must also say it is a sin, because it destroys God's creation and God's economy for sexuality.

Is there any Biblical instruction regarding transgenderism? There are no direct verses condemning transgenderism in the Scripture. We see, however, in the Book of Genesis how the Bible speaks about two biological sexes and genders, male and female.[8] But there is a passage, although it does not directly speak about transgenderism, if we understand it correctly, then we can understand that this passage is also hinting at the sin of transgenderism.

In the Book of Deuteronomy, the Bible speaks about cross-dressing, saying, "A woman shall not wear anything that pertains to a man, nor shall a man put on a woman's garment, for all who do so are an

---

8   See Genesis 1–2.

abomination to the LORD your God."[9] If a male dresses like a female or a female dresses like a male, this is an abomination to the Lord. We know for sure that the transgender movement goes beyond just wearing clothes that make one appear to be of the opposite gender. They do not stop at this; rather, they take hormones, they have surgeries, and so on. But let us understand why this verse came. Understanding that within the Israelite culture, there was a certain style of dress with ornaments or items that distinguished men and women, we understand that this verse firstly means that everyone needed to let their gender expression align with their biological sex. Because if I am a male, dressed like a female, then my gender expression is different from my biological sex.

Secondly, everyone needed to guard against gender confusion because if a male dressed like a female or a female dressed like a male, this would cause gender confusion. And God does not accept gender confusion; it is an abomination to God. This commandment says that you need to affirm your biological sex, which means that the expression of your gender should be consistent with your biological sex. And, as I said, this verse ended with a very strong word: an abomination to the Lord. "A woman shall not wear anything that pertains to a man, nor shall a man put on a woman's garment, for all who do so are an abomination to the LORD your God."[10]

---

9   Deuteronomy 22:5.
10   Deuteronomy 22:5.

The same term "abomination" is used with sins like idolatry, wickedness, and sexual sins. So these great violations against the Law of God are abominations. So we are surprised that the same word "abomination" that is used with sins like worshipping idols, fornication, idolatry, and living in wickedness, the same word is applied just for gender confusion, if a man wears a woman's dress or the opposite.

If we try to understand why this is an abomination to the Lord, it is because it violates God's ordered connection between biological sex and gender expression. God takes it very seriously that the human beings whom He created are to express themselves in keeping with how He made them biologically. God wants us to express ourselves exactly like our biological sex.

Here we would like to address another point. I said, "Should we let the mind align to the body or the body to the mind?" The transgender person wants the body to align with the mind. But this has a false theological understanding, that the body is not good, so it is okay to destroy your body, but not your mind. So there is a disconnect in the transgender debate between mind and body. The most common solution to the gender dysphoria—dysphoria meaning I am not comfortable with my biological sex—is to bring the body into alignment with the mind rather than bringing the mind into alignment with the body. And in doing so, when they destroy their body, this means the body is less valuable than the mind.

But if we understand, again, God's economy, we will understand that the body is a very important piece of God's good creation, as is the mind. After God created the world, each day ended with "And God saw that it was good," until the sixth day. On the sixth day, there were two proclamations. The first one, "It was good,"[11] and then God repeated, saying, "Then God saw everything that He had made, and indeed it was very good."[12] So for the sixth day, in which Adam and Eve were created, there were two proclamations, the first one said, "God saw that it was good," and the second one said, "And indeed it was very good."

God created the corporeal aspect of the universe, and then He declared it to be good on the five days. What God created is good. Yes, as we read in Genesis 3, when sin entered the world, it destroyed the goodness that God created in His creation, but God's creation is good. Yes, the fall corrupted our physical being, but even with this corruption, it did not corrupt our physical being to the point that we are unable to recognize its goodness. No, until now, we can see the goodness of the body and God's creation.

I remember when I was in medical school, studying physiology, our professor was not Christian, but several times when he was explaining, for example, the physiology of the eye or the physiology of the liver and the metabolism, he would pause and say, "See the

---

11 Genesis 1:25.
12 Genesis 1:31.

greatness of the Creator! See how God created us in a very unique and wise way!" After 7000 years from the creation of Adam and Eve, we do not see that there has been another version of humanity created that is an updated version. In phones and computers, we have version 1, version 2, version 3, and so on, because they always need improvement. But the creation of the human being, from Adam and Eve until now, has not needed any improvement.

In Psalm 139, David reflected beautifully on the creation of the body and said:

> For You formed my inward parts; You covered me in my mother's womb. I will praise You, for I am fearfully and wonderfully made; marvelous are Your works, and that my soul knows very well. My frame was not hidden from You, when I was made in secret, and skillfully wrought in the lowest parts of the earth. Your eyes saw my substance, being yet unformed. And in Your book, they all were written, the days fashioned for me, when as yet there were none of them.[13]

The work of God—and how He created our human body—is amazing, exceedingly above and beyond our understanding. So our bodies are not random parts, just put together haphazardly; no, they are the purposeful work of God's hands. They are not only good but are

---

13   Psalms 139:13–16.

very good. Unfortunately, many beliefs demean the body and speak of the body as being less important than the mind or the spirit. But in the Bible, we know that not only is the body the good creation of God, but it is a gift from God to us.

By making the body align to the mind, we are demeaning the goodness of the body and destroying the goodness of the body that God created purposefully. Such elevation of the mind over the body will result in a denial of the goodness of the physical body. This is a gnostic approach, which says that there is a tension between our true selves and our bodies. So the idea that our true self is different from the body, in which we live, communicates that our body is something less than us and can be used or shamed or changed to match what we feel; and this is Gnosticism. Taking a gnostic approach towards mind-body discomfort or tension, regarding sexuality and gender, will lead to more confusion over gender in our society, ultimately resulting in the erasing of all gender distinctions.

Knowing this, it is important to think about how we should honor our bodies. "Your body is the temple of the Holy Spirit who is in you."[14] You are the temple of God, and the Holy Spirit abides in you.

So let us address how to respond to the transgender sin. The main point here is that our responses until now have been reactive and not proactive. And sometimes it is combative, as if we are fighting, not

---

14   1 Corinthians 6:19.

compassionate. And we sometimes become defensive when we are defending God's economy for sexuality, not responding in a way to disciple, to make others disciples of Christ. That is why we need to respond to the transgender debate in a way that encourages people and moves them to embrace the goodness of the creation of God, to be disciples of God, and to end by worshipping God who created us beautifully as males and females. So our response should be proactive, not reactive; compassionate, not combative; and discipling, not defensive, to make them disciples of Christ.

How do we achieve this? Unfortunately, our society is now justifying what is wrong and evil as normal and good. And as I explained, they are separating gender and sex. They are saying people are born biologically as male and female, but this is not necessarily their gender identity. If a person is not comfortable with their biological sex, they call it gender dysphoria. And the word dysphoria means unease or dissatisfaction. So I am not satisfied with the biological sex I was born with.

There are two categories for gender dysphoria: early-onset gender dysphoria and rapid gender dysphoria. The early-onset gender dysphoria, the child feels like he is the opposite sex from the age of 2-4 years. This is very rare and caused by parenting mistakes. They are not born like this. I know now they are trying to do some medical research to support the claim that they are born like this, but no, these studies are neither accurate nor credible. It is mainly caused by parenting mistakes. But just to give you a very small example: a mother, because she wanted to have a girl but has a boy, who is two or three years old, grows his hair and makes him have long hair. And many people, when they see this boy, think he is a girl. It happened to me. I was visiting a family, and I saw a little girl. I thought she was a girl. And they told me, "No, he is a boy." They started this gender confusion for this boy, and that is why it scares me when I see a young boy growing his hair. And the parents do not understand that this can lead to gender confusion and gender dysphoria and transgenderism in the future. You may tell me, "This has been happening for many years, but they grow normal. Why is it different now?" Because the society around us is marketing transgenderism as an alternative lifestyle. Before, they would say it was wrong. But now, society, school, cartoons, movies, and social media are conveying the message that it is cool to be transgender. That is why it is growing. That is the first type.

The second type is called rapid gender dysphoria. It affects teens and adults. They identify themselves with biological sex until they become adolescents or adults, 15 or 16 years old, where they decide to change their gender. So a boy wants to be a girl, or the opposite. The main cause of the rapid gender dysphoria in adolescence is social media, because it is celebrating transgenderism. Some youth—not all youth—choose this path to follow and be transgender because they are seeking attention and popularity. This is especially the case if they suffer from low self-esteem, anxiety, depression, eating disorders, personality disorders, self-injury, sexual trauma, or genital trauma. These things make these youth have the potential to go down the path of gender dysphoria.

In God's creation, the body should submit to the soul or the spirit, and the spirit should submit to the Holy Spirit of God. But this submission does not mean that one is inferior or better than the other. When the Bible says about the Son, that the Son will submit to the Father, this does not mean that the Father is higher than the Son or that the Son is lower than the Father.[15] No, it is not so. St. Paul said, "I discipline my body and bring it into subjection."[16] Because if the body is not disciplined, then the desires of the body can lead the soul and the spirit into a lower state, not being connected with God. When we do not follow this order—that the body should submit to the spirit, and the spirit should submit to the Spirit of God—we cannot function properly.

This is the order, like in marriage when God said, "Wives, submit to your own husbands,"[17] this does not mean that she is less. And we see in marriage that when a wife submits to her husband, the marriage becomes successful. And the husband submits to the Spirit of

---

15   See 1 Corinthians 15:28.

16   1 Corinthians 9:27.

17   Ephesians 5:22.

God—again, the same order. But when there is a power struggle between the husband and the wife, and there is no submission to the order and the Holy Spirit, then many problems ensue in the family. Nevertheless, this does not mean that wives are less than husbands. It is the same way when we say that the body is good, but it does not mean that the body should lead the spirit or should lead the Holy Spirit. The body should submit to the spirit, and the spirit to the Holy Spirit.

2

Dealing with Transgenderism

We are speaking now about how to help people with transgenderism. I will address four points:

1. How to help the people who have already undergone the surgeries and now want to repent.

2. How to help the people who are considering doing the surgeries.

3. How to help the parents who come to you concerning their children who are claiming to be transgender.

4. Some preventive measures, in order to be proactive, not reactive.

Also, I will try to respond to the question of how we should deal with transgender people at work and school, who are asking us to use a certain pronoun, and so on. How do we handle this? Of course, there are some common principles for all these different categories, and there are specific principles for each category. Let us start with some common principles.

Learning to Embrace My Physical Body from Childhood

I think the first thing is that we need to teach people from childhood how to embrace their physical body, even if there is discomfort or dissatisfaction with their physical body. Teaching about the goodness of the physical world in general, and our bodies in particular, is a very crucial point and shows a commitment to honor God's creation. We should know that we are not just bodies, but rather, we are embodied souls. What do I mean by embodied souls? Souls that are living in this body. And both components are good and created by God. So we are composed of both a material body and an immaterial soul. As we read in Genesis, God created the body first from the dust, then He breathed into this body the spirit.

The body and the soul become integrated into a unified whole. It is sometimes described as psychosomatic unity. The union of the body and the soul describes the complex nature of humanity. But this complexity is designed by God to function in unity. There is harmony between my body and my soul. Both function in unity. Perceiving myself as God created me, as an embodied soul, means that I am committed to the economy of God and the creation of God—that both of them are good: the material and the immaterial components of myself.

29

There are two extremes. Some people embrace the goodness of the physical body but do not do so to the same extent with the soul. They undermine the immaterial component of humanity—the soul. As I said in the previous chapter, Gnosticism elevates the immaterial, whether it is the soul or the mind, over the material. Both extremes are wrong, however. We cannot adopt either of these extremes, but we need to balance both the material and immaterial, the body and the soul. And when it comes to the biological sex and gender, God's design is that they are a unified whole, affirming one another. God does not create us in dissociation, the body being dissociated from the soul or mind. God would certainly not do this. God is not a God of chaos; He is the God of order, as we read in chapter eleven of the first epistle to the Corinthians.

Asking About the Underlying Causes of Gender Confusion

When the cognitive discomfort of gender confusion appears, we, as counselors or servants or parents or clergy, need to begin by asking the question of what is causing the discomfort. Why is this child or adolescent having this dissatisfaction? In many cases, as I said in the first chapter, they are perhaps seeking attention or acting upon a perceived cultural expression of sexuality that is popular right now: it is cool to be transgender. Or there may be some roots deeper than this: maybe a mistake in parenting, sexual trauma, or genital trauma.

We must not take these things lightly. Instead, we need to walk alongside these individuals and let them share with us their psychological understanding of who they are, why they think the way they are thinking, and why there is discomfort. And then, gradually, we need to affirm to them the goodness of the body and also the goodness of the soul, and how it is in the best interest of humanity that God created both of them to align with each other and to work in harmony with each other, not to dissociate one from the other.

Preventive Measures

So we need to establish in our kids, as part of preventive measures, a secure and stable sexual identity that is designed by God. Many times parents do not raise their children according to their proper sex: for example, like growing the hair, letting them play with boys' toys or girls' toys, and the way they dress them. For example, boys may be dressed as females, or girls may be dressed in male attire. Or sometimes a boy has only sisters—or a girl has only brothers—even most of the friends of the family may be girls—or most of them may be boys. So we need to pay attention to this boy or this girl, raising them in a different way than the other boys and girls.

Also, we need to initiate an early onset age-appropriate sex education at home and church. It is better to teach our children at church and at home before they learn from outside. You will be surprised when you know that kids as early as six years old are aware of homosexuality and transgenderism. That is why we need to address these issues in our homes and in our churches in an age-appropriate way. We need to teach our children before they get exposed to the sexually immoral world we are living in today.

Simply, for example, if you are reading the story of creation to your children at three or four years of age, you can introduce the word "gender" and say that there are only two genders, male and female. And marriage is between a male and a female. So here, you are planting these principles in their minds: God created a male and a female, and these are the only two genders; there are no other genders. Marriage is between a male and a female, because two males cannot reproduce. You can ask the child, "Why did God create a male and a female? Why did He not create two Adams or two Eves?" And you can lead him or her to answer this question by saying, "Because they complement one another." You can plant these theological principles in their minds, even if they are two or three years old, in a simple question-and-answer manner. So when they grow up, they do not believe that there are twenty-six other genders.

And you need to make your children, whether Sunday school children or biological children, proud of their gender, and you can give them examples. St. Mary is proud to be a female; she became the Mother of God. Moses was proud to be a male, and I am proud to be a male. Or one can say, "I am proud to be a female." Use this and emphasize this repeatedly with your children, even when they pray, teaching them to thank God for creating them the gender that they are, as a man or a woman or a boy or a girl.

Listen to Them

If your child comes to you, saying, "I want to be transgender," or "I have a friend in school; she is a girl and now he is a boy," do not shut them down. Do not say, "No, no, no! We do not have this in our faith." And sometimes, when you say that we do not have this in our faith or our church or our culture, what we are teaching them is that this belief is not an absolute belief; it is related to this culture or related to this faith. So, you are encouraging them unintentionally to change their faith: "Maybe if I change my faith, then I can change this belief." Listen to them; let them speak in order to understand their reasoning behind why they are fascinated, wanting to convert to the other gender. You need to understand what the factors are that lead your child or even an adolescent to this. Why do they want to change their gender?

What is the Cause?

1. **A Child-Parent Disconnect**. Many times, a breakdown in the child's family, like abandonment by the father or the mother, can be the reason. For example, in homosexuality, they find in many cases that the reason is the absence of a connection between

the child and the parent of the same gender, a boy with the father or a girl with the mother. This disconnection is either because the father is busy or is travelling all the time, or because of a conflict or a divorce in the family, and so on.

When we are children, there is a time when boys are attracted to boys, and girls are attracted to girls. And then, when they start adolescence, the reverse happens: boys start to get attracted to girls, and girls start to get attracted to boys. But if a boy is disconnected from his father or if a girl is disconnected from her mother, what will happen is that the world of manhood or the world of womanhood is completely unclear to the child. So, subconsciously, he wants to connect with men, or a girl wants to connect with women. This may be to replace the mother figure or father figure in their life, or just to explore this world, the world of men or the world of women, because we build this experience through our connection with our parents. I learn mainly about the world of men from my father. And I learn about the world of women from my mother. This is how it starts. And then, if I want to explore this world and have moved into the age of adolescence, and the hormones start to kick in during this time, this attraction to the world of men or the world of women, with the hormones, makes it a sexual attraction, and that is how homosexuality starts. The same applies to transgenderism. Because this world is obscured. So if I perhaps change from this gender to that gender, then I can explore this world better.

All these are not calculated mental decisions, but it is a subconscious exploration of this world. And again, someone might say, "But why did this not happen 50 years ago, although there were conflicts between parents and children?" Because the option of transgenderism or homosexuality was not there. The whole world, whether they were Christian or not—atheist or secular or religious—said that this is an abnormality. Even in earlier editions of the DSM (Diagnostic and Statistical Manual of Mental Disorders), these were considered a deviation from the normal sexuality and considered an illness that needed treatment. Now, in the DSM-5, they do not label it as an illness anymore; they consider it an alternative lifestyle. It became acceptable. That is why this shift, which happened in our culture to support the LGBTQ community, made it easier for girls or boys to say, "I am transgender," or "I am homosexual," and now they are supported by laws from the country, and so on.

2. Abuse. Another reason, when you ask your child why they want to change their gender, may be that they were rejected or abused, and it may be that their friends from school made fun of their gender at school. For example, for a boy, if he is soft-spoken, they make fun of him and say that he is a female. And for a girl, if she has brothers and she acts in school like a boy, they make fun of her gender, so this can lead to dissatisfaction with their biological sex.

3. Gender Discrimination. Another reason is gender discrimination. If I see my parents treating my brothers better than me because I am a girl, or even in school, or in the culture (in some cultures, they prefer boys over girls), the discrimination can lead a person to say, "I want to be a male to get these privileges and this freedom." Believe me, even here in America, I see some families give unconditional, unlimited freedom to their boys, with no rules for the boys, but for the girls, there are many restrictions. So, this gender discrimination can be a reason why they want to change their gender.

4. **Mental Illness**. Also, the child might be suffering from a mental or personality disorder. Professional help here can help in diagnosing very early if there is a personality disorder or mental illness that is contributing to this.

5. **Pornography**. You also need to check if your children were exposed to pornography. This can also affect them, especially if they are watching pornography of homosexuality or pornography in which women are oppressed and abused. So a female might hate the female gender, because she sees in this pornography how women are abused and taken advantage of. And perhaps they want to be males just to see how in pornography males are presented as stronger, more powerful, overcoming, and so on.

6. **Pressure by Society**. The cause may simply be that it is the pressure from the LGBTQ community and how they influence the child in one way or another, like through social media, cartoons, friends, and so on. It is just cool to be a transgender or homosexual person.

How do we Address Transgenderism?

If it is a sin, then before we speak about psychological help or professional help, we need to build a relationship with God, because any help for the transgender or homosexual person, without building a relationship with God, will fail. You can give them a list of rules that they may follow from the outside, but the heart will not change. "Do not dress like this; do not walk in this way; stay away from these friends." You can give them a set of rules, but this will not be successful for people struggling with their gender, because we are simply emphasizing the proper gender expression that leads to socially acceptable behavior, but without a change of heart. So when they find an opportunity to rebel against all these rules or commands, they will rebel against them. So these commands can include dressing in a gender-specific way, wearing a gender-specific hairstyle, pursuing gender-specific activities, and so on.

Here, we are training people to be hypocrites, to be something different on the inside than what they are on the outside. This is like how the Lord described the Pharisees and the religious leaders of Israel, as white-washed tombs. He said, "Woe to you, scribes and Pharisees, hypocrites! For you are like whitewashed tombs which indeed appear beautiful outwardly,"— Yes, my sexual expression fits exactly the norm of society—"but inside are full of dead men's bones and all uncleanness."[18] From inside, I am not pure. In the same way, on the outside you seem righteous to people, but inside you are full of hypocrisy and lawlessness. Taking this rule-based approach, we want to shape them into this gender without changing their heart. That is why the right approach is to start by changing the heart. And when the heart is changed, then the external expression will also change. This begins with an acknowledgement of sin, repentance, confession, and worshipping the Lord faithfully and righteously.

The first step here is the acknowledgement that it is a sin. And sin needs to be repented of. Sin needs to be confessed. Sin needs to be overcome through a strong relationship with the Lord. We need to guide the people into devoting their lives to worship the Creator who created them in this gender in this way. I am no longer worshipping the culture or the community, nor am I seeking the approval of men. Rather, I am worshipping the Creator who created me very uniquely, very purposefully, very good in this gender and sex.

As we read in the Bible, "Therefore, whether you eat or drink, or whatever you do, do all to the glory of God."[19] So every aspect of our life is focused on bringing glory to God. This is the road of discipleship. As the Lord said to us, "If you want to be my disciple."[20] As a disciple of the Lord, I will obey His commandments

18   Matthew 23:27–28.
19   1 Corinthians 10:31.
20   Luke 14:25–33.

and His expectations of me, and this expectation includes my gender. The expression of gender here to match the biological sex will not be just an act of duty or following a set of commandments, but rather it will be an expression of love toward my Creator and my Savior. This will lead to a complete change of who you are from the inside to outside.

Because the Scripture is clear that all of us have fallen under the influence of sin, that sin entered the world, and all of us are impacted by sin, even if we do not struggle with transgenderism, our personal struggles are real. Maybe I am struggling with anger; maybe I am struggling with lust. Without this repentance and returning to God, it will be impossible for me to overcome these struggles. Yes, I am aware of my weaknesses and my struggles, but I also have confidence that the Lord Jesus Christ has redeemed me from the power of sin, including any sin of a sexual nature. As St. Paul said, "And such were some of you, [fornicators, adulterers, homosexuals, transgenders].[21] But you were washed, but you were sanctified, but you were justified in the name of the Lord Jesus and by the Spirit of our God."[22]

We are no longer identified by our sinful struggle. So if I am struggling with transgenderism, I am not identified as transgender. This cannot and will not identify who I am. But I am identified by the

---

21 See 1 Corinthians 6:10 for the text in brackets.

22 1 Corinthians 6:11.

redemptive act of God, my Lord Jesus Christ. Because if I am identified by my sinful struggle, this means my struggle will never disappear, because now it identifies me, now it has victory over me. If I say, "I am homosexual," or "I am transgender," then I permit this sin to overcome me and to have victory over me.

Addressing transgenderism with parents or children or adolescents or even little children, we need to use the theological foundation that is the foundation upon which we will build our discussion, and by identifying the theological foundation that drives our understanding of who we are, we will find that transgenderism is a disordering of God's design for sexuality. God ordered sexuality in a certain way. Transgenderism and homosexuality are disordering the design of God. What is the tool I am using to disorder the design of God? I am using the body, which is also God's design. He called it good in the Book of Genesis, and after He created humanity, God looked at it and said that it was very good.

Without having a conversion to be devoted to God, to be devoted to the Church, and to become disciples of Christ, we cannot overcome these sins. Parents and the Church should teach about the beauty and goodness of the whole creation, of our bodies and souls, and the unified whole of the embodied soul, and how the body and soul work together in harmony. This teaching should lead us to gratefulness, gratitude, and thanksgiving to God.

We must be committed to walking alongside people who are struggling with their gender identity, without condemning them or judging them. For we certainly know that God loves them; He died on the Cross for them. He has an order of creation designed for their lives, and He has a plan for their healing and recovery. We need to trust that God can heal them completely. Like the man who said to the Lord, "Say the word, and my servant will be healed."[23] We need to have this trust that God can heal them completely.

In the culture we live in, in our society, we need to stand by our commitment to support those who create laws and the politicians who affirm God's design for gender and sexuality. In voting, we need to again support those who affirm God's design for gender and sexuality. So, in summary, we need to instill in them the love of God before we teach the same morality, or a certain discipline, or a particular course of action. When we learn to love God, we will automatically desire to keep His commandments. We need to instill in our children the need to honor God more than people and more than the pressure from people around us.

Also, we need to teach our children to take their gender roles from the Scripture and not from society. What are the roles assigned to males, and what are the roles assigned to females? We need to take this from the Scripture, not from society. Even beyond the

---

23 Luke 7:7.

41

issue of gender identity, not respecting God's order is invading the Church, for example, the priesthood of women. This is again not following God's order. If God wants women to be clergy, in the Old Testament He would have chosen women to be priests from among the descendants or children of Aaron; or in the New Testament, He would have assigned some women to be among the twelve disciples and He would have breathed on some women, saying, "Receive the Holy Spirit," and given them the authority to forgive sins, and to bind and to loose as He did with the disciples.

But again, because of the pressure of the feminist movement, now we are fighting against the idea that women do not read in church. And they would say, "They read better than boys." Yes, I know many females read better than boys, but the rank of Reader has been assigned for 2000 years to boys, not to anybody. And, in the Church, only those who can read are the Readers, not the regular man in church who is not ordained as a Reader; such a man must not read in church, even if he reads very well. But we are trying to push deaconship on females and are trying to challenge the role that God assigned to men and women. And let us see the impact of this on our families.

When families respected the roles assigned to men and the roles assigned to women, we had families that had twelve or fifteen children just thirty or forty years ago, and all of them were raised in a godly manner, and were healthy, physically and mentally. We did not hear about panic attacks, anxiety, hurting themselves, or cutting themselves. We did not hear about all of these. But once we started to confuse the roles of men and women, even in parenting, even within the household, look and see our society right now, how it looks! Most of the youth are suffering from anxiety, panic attacks, and cutting. Most of the families have two children. Many of them, unfortunately, suffer from these stress disorders and anxiety. Why is all of this? Because we are disordering God's economy. We want to impose our philosophy and our understanding on God's plan and God's economy.

If women want to do everything men do, why did He create two genders? But that is what we are doing now. The confusion between equality and difference in roles is an illness in our society. They say that a difference in roles means that they are not equal. This has led to a rise in the number of divorce cases, the number of children suffering from personality disorders, and so on. Let us respect the roles of the two genders that God assigned, and let us take the gender roles from the Scripture and not from society. And let us not impose what society is teaching on the Church or our families. Believe me, this will destroy our families and our children. And the saddest thing here is that we are blind to this. We are blind to the negative effects of not respecting the gender roles in the Scripture and following society's gender roles.

The Scripture is very clear that both male and female are equally valuable in the eyes of God. They have different roles, but they complement one another.

St. Paul spoke about this in detail in his first epistle to the Corinthians, when he was speaking about the gifts of the Spirit. He said, "If the foot should say, 'Because I am not a hand, I am not of the body,' is it therefore not of the body? And if the ear should say, 'Because I am not an eye, I am not of the body,' is it therefore not of the body? If the whole body were an eye, where would be the hearing?... And if they were all one member, where would the body be?"[24] If the ear said, "Why am I not the eye?" and the eye said, "Why am I not the ear?" the body will not function. We need to explain this very early to our children.

Men are created for certain roles, and women are created for certain roles, and these roles complement each other. God made our bodies, our souls, and our minds to perform these roles. Also, we need to teach how to deal with, honor, and respect the other gender. We need to teach boys how to respect girls, and girls how to respect boys. And of course, we as parents need to stay away from gender discrimination. And we should know that our identity is in Christ. If I am struggling, as I said, we need to put this struggle in prayer before God. As St. Paul said, "Be anxious for nothing, but in everything by prayer and supplication, with thanksgiving, let your requests be made known to God; and the peace of God, which surpasses all understanding, will guard your hearts and minds through Christ Jesus."[25] We need to be confident that

24   1 Corinthians 12:15–17, 19.

25   Philippians 4:6–7.

God can completely heal the person. So we need to enter into a genuine and sincere relationship with God.

Also, we need to maintain an eternal mindset, for us and for our children; as St. Paul said, "If then you were raised with Christ, seek those things which are above,"[26] not on things below. And disordering God's creation, this abomination to the Lord, will be punished eternally as a sin if the person does not repent. So then part of "I want to reach my eternity, to be with Christ," is that I need to respect and honor God in His order of creation. The more they respect their gender and respect the gender of the other sex, the more they will be connected with God, and the more they will understand their role and purpose.

What if a person who is Coptic Orthodox claims that the Word of God has no authority, or that he does not believe in God, or that he is an atheist right now? All my discussion is based on the Scripture, the authority of the Scripture, and the infallibility of the Scripture. But the easiest challenge this person might make is by saying, "What if the Scripture is wrong? What if this is the opinion of St. Paul, not the opinion of God? What if the Scripture is not inspired?" And this is one of the attacks of the devil, to cast doubt on the inspiration, the authenticity, and the authority of the Scripture.

We need, here, to present God to them from the experience of godly people. You can tell them, "Yes, I

---

26 Colossians 3:1.

understand you do not believe in the Scripture. You do not believe in the authority of the Scripture, but let us look at history and see people who believed in the Scripture, what their life looked like, and people who did not believe in the Scripture of God, how their life looked." Do not make them look bad and do not make them feel bad, but present God to them from the experience of godly people. And tell them, "What if you just try God? You say you do not believe in Him, so you are not going to lose anything if you try this and that, while you are still struggling. If you are told, 'There is a new medicine; try it,' you will try it."

I know people, for example, who are suffering from cancer, and they seek clinical trials. Clinical trials mean that the medicine has not been proven yet. And they seek clinical trials with the hope that it may work for them. So, consider it as a clinical trial. Although I, as a parent or as a servant, know it is 100% true. But for them, just let them consider accepting God. So invite them, as David said in the Psalms, "Oh, taste and see that the LORD is good."[27]

I like the story of Philip and Nathanael. When Nathanael started to have the question, "Can anything good come out of Nazareth?"[28] Philip responded to him with three words, "Come and see."[29] Come and see—try. And when he took him to the Lord, his whole life was changed. He did not only believe that

27 Psalms 34:8.
28 John 1:46.
29 Ibid.

Jesus was a prophet or a good person—he could not believe at first that something good would come out of Nazareth—but he believed and made a confession, saying, "You are the Son of God! You are the King of Israel!"[30] So just let them have an experience with God.

I remember talking with an atheist, and after a long discussion about many questions he had, I told him, "Just try for the next ten days, two weeks, three weeks; just pray to God to reveal Himself to you. If there is a God and He reveals Himself to you, then you know the truth. But if, as you said, there is no God, then you are praying to nothing, so you are not going to lose anything. You are not going to hurt yourself. So for you, it is a win-win situation." And by the way, he is a professor of philosophy at a university. I was surprised by his answer, for he told me, "I know if I pray, I will believe." So I told him, "Then you choose not to believe." And he said to me, "If that is how you look at it, you can look at it in this way." Just invite them to experience God, even if they do not believe in Him, just like a clinical trial, as I said. Just try. Come and see, come and taste the Lord.

St. Paul made it very clear in his first epistle to the Corinthians that your body is not your own. And if my body is not my own, then I should not alter my body; I have no authority over my body. He said, "Do you not know that your body is the temple of the Holy Spirit who is in you, whom you have from God,

---

30   John 1:49.

47

and you are not your own? For you were bought at a price; therefore glorify God in your body and in your spirit, which are God's."[31] So the question here is, am I glorifying God in my body if I am taking all these hormones and doing these surgeries? He said, "You were bought at a price, you are not your own." I have no authority over my body. I should take care of it, nurture it, and discipline it to glorify God. My body should be honored and respected and used to glorify God, not to disorder the order of God.

For example, if you go to an art gallery and purchase a picture painted by an artist at an expensive price, who will dare to alter the picture with their own editing? No one. What about your body? To alter your body through hormone therapy or changing the genitalia is a form of denying God, denying that I am His masterpiece. So it is a denial of God.

One of the physicians who is not a Christian made it very clear that you cannot change a male to a female and a female to a male. You cannot. You can just make external expressions, but you cannot change a male to a female. Because changing the genitalia or appearance or hormones does not change the person's sex DNA. You will continue to be female regardless of the alterations made. Do not change God's original design for your life. God will hold you accountable as male and female. Saturate your mind with the truth, the Word of God.

---

31   1 Corinthians 6:19–20.

The Six Stages of Change

Change has six stages. For example, if you are dealing with a person who is transgender and you are trying to lead them in the right way, you need to first determine which stage they are at, because based on their stage, you will deal with them. And there are six stages. The first one is unwillingness, so you may meet a person who is not willing to change: "I believe I am a female when I am a male." The second stage is dreaming: "Yes, I know I am wrong, but it is impossible for me to change back or to align my mind with my body or to feel that I am a male." The third stage is willingness. The person is willing to make the change and to repent, and they may have started to have some plans. The fourth stage is acting. They are acting on their repentance and how to return to be male or female according to their biological sex. The fifth stage is persevering. There is tension, but I am struggling, so I am persevering. And the last stage is recovery. Now, the person is completely recovered.

The First Stage: Unwillingness

How do I deal with a person who is at this stage? I am dealing with a person who is not willing. For example, if parents tell me that their son is considering transgenderism or he is saying that he is a girl, and you meet with him, and he has all these reasons why he thinks that he is a female and not a male. And he is very much convinced and is not willing to consider it a sin and to repent, nor is he willing to consider it an illness. He is seeing it as an alternative, normal lifestyle. How do you deal with this person?

First, you need to understand why. What are his reasons? And while you are listening to him, you need to diagnose the wrong beliefs, because he is convinced that he is a female based on certain beliefs, and these beliefs are wrong. For example, he may tell you, "I am a female imprisoned in a male body, but that is who I am." So you need to identify these false beliefs, and then discuss them with him from a Biblical perspective using the authority of the Bible, sound reason, and sound science and medicine.

Maybe he is not willing, because in his mind, it is impossible for the change to happen. One transgender person told me, "I tried. I went to many counselors, many psychiatrists. I tried my best. I went to monasteries. I prayed and asked God to change me, but it is impossible for me to change, so the only solution I have is to accept who I am. I tried for years." He definitely tried for years, but never tried the right thing. If I am trying the wrong medicine, I will not be healed. Or I may be trying externally, but not from my heart. I am trying because of the pressure from my family. And this person told me that while he was in Egypt before coming to America, his family would beat him. He tried to change in response to this violence from the family, not because he wanted to change. And this violence created more resistance and more rebellion in his heart. You cannot solve these issues by beating your son or daughter.

And you need to acknowledge the reality of their feelings. Acknowledging it and understanding it do not mean that you are agreeing with or approving of it. For example, there is a difference between saying, "There is nothing called you are a male imprisoned in a female body. That is nonsense!" which of course will immediately create resistance, but you ought to acknowledge it, and this is what we call empathy, saying to him, "Yes, I understand you feel that you are a male imprisoned in a female body. I understand this." So understanding does not mean you approve that this is normal, but this will assure him that he is not crazy because his feelings are true to him.

Then, you can tell him, "If a person has anorexia, for example, what would we do? Are we going to align the mind to the body or the body to the mind?" So you need to address these things with him and tell him, "I believe that your feelings are real to you; that is how you feel. But the solution you are seeking is not the right thing to do. When people suffer from anorexia, they feel they are overweight. Are they right? When a young girl insists that she is a mermaid, are we going to throw her into the sea because she said she is a mermaid? If you feel younger, does this mean you have a different age? If you feel taller, does this mean you have a different height? Why does gender rely on feeling, but not race, age, or height? And instead of feeling like you are a woman trapped in a man's body, why do you not feel that you are a man with a woman's mind?" So instead of saying I am a woman trapped in a man's body, you can acknowledge his feelings by saying, "Yes, I understand you are saying you are a man with a woman's mind." What I am trying to say here is that you need to acknowledge his feelings. Because if you do not acknowledge his feelings and understand them, you are creating resistance. You are building a barrier between you and him.

Also, the self-perception that I am a woman or I am a man serves a certain purpose in my life. Maybe it gives them the attention they need or the satisfaction they need. So you need to identify what purposes are served by their self-perception and how we can satisfy these needs in a healthy way, in a godly way, in the proper way. Yes, we understand them, but we will not enable them. But rather, we need to speak the truth in love. We need to say, "This is a sin." They need to repent, as all of us are sinners. I have my own sins that I am struggling with, and I need to repent. Therefore, do not talk to them as a righteous man speaking to a sinner. And you need to emphasize that you, too, are a sinner. Maybe you are struggling with transgenderism, but I am struggling with anger, and it is the same because "Whoever shall keep the whole law, and yet stumble in one point, he is guilty of all."[32]

But in the end, you cannot help someone who refuses to get help. We will continue with these people who are refusing to get help with three things: prayer, not enabling them, and gentle confrontation, speaking

---

32   James 2:10.

the truth in love. Prayer means praying to God that He may change their heart; Do not enable means do not support them in the wrong way; and gentle confrontation means every now and then you need to confront them gently, speaking the truth in love.

The Second Stage: Dreaming

If they are in the second stage, which is the dreaming stage, they know it is a sin, but they believe it is impossible to overcome this sin. Therefore, these people need support from God and need to strengthen their faith in the Lord. One of the most beautiful verses for these people is in the epistle to the Romans. St. Paul says, "But if the Spirit of Him who raised Jesus from the dead dwells in you, He who raised Christ from the dead will also give life to your mortal bodies through His Spirit who dwells in you."[33] Is it possible for someone who died for three days to rise from the dead? No, it is impossible. But we have Jesus who rose from the dead, and He arose by the work of the Trinity. As St. Paul said that if the same Spirit of Him who raised Jesus from the dead dwells in you, then the Holy Spirit who raised Jesus from the dead will also give life to your mortal bodies, "through His Spirit who dwells in you."

So if they lost all hope, I would ask this question, "Do you have this Holy Spirit in you?" Yes, we received the Holy Spirit after Baptism. The Holy

33   Romans 8:11.

Spirit is abiding in me. You are the temple of God, and the Holy Spirit abides in you. What did the Holy Spirit do? He raised the Lord Jesus from the dead. Is it impossible to be raised from the dead? Yes, it is impossible. The Holy Spirit was able to do this with Jesus, and He did this through Jesus with Lazarus, and He did this through St. Paul with Eutyches. We have many stories of how the Holy Spirit raised people from the dead, which is impossible, which is hopeless and helpless. And you have the same Spirit; then yes, you can rise from the deadness of transgenderism.

Give them hope, encourage them, and share real stories of recovered transgender people. And there are real stories. I just shared with you the story of this person who, after being transgender and even getting married for fifteen years, the Holy Spirit worked in him, and he is living a beautiful life of repentance. So, in the stage of dreaming, what do they need? They need encouragement and hope to get them out of their hopelessness; hope not in themselves, trust not in themselves, but trust in God, the Holy Spirit who raised Jesus from the dead.

The Third Stage: Willingness

The third stage is willingness. I think many people say, "Yes, I will," but they do not have practical action plans. So, with people who are willing, you need to discuss their plans with them. What are you going to do? For example, if I am willing, but I still watch pornography, then I am not willing. If I am willing, but I still have not built my relationship with Christ, and I do not pray, and I do not go to church, and I am not living a life of repentance, then I am not willing. For, as I told you, you cannot overcome this without the grace of God.

Perhaps reconciliation with their parents, with their families, with their siblings, for example, can be a step here in their willingness; or perhaps avoiding a group of friends or turning off all social media, because they have a negative impact on them. After I first understand the reasons, the action plan should be directed toward these reasons. So discuss the action plan with them. Set clear goals. What is their goal? When they say, "I am willing," willing to do what? Maybe they are just willing to change the external sexual expression. Willing here means they will change their attire, but their heart is still sick. This should not be the goal.

And you need to discuss with them whether they have a support system or not. And we have two support systems: the visible and the invisible support systems. The visible support system is the church, godly friends in the church, the priest, my father of confession, and spiritually mature servants; and I can also include the family, especially if the family understands how they are dysfunctional or discriminate against a certain gender or negatively treat their children with violence, for example, as I just explained. Or maybe they are disconnected from their children because of the busyness. So, counseling provided to the family to be supportive of their children will also help. I usually say that the best two visible support systems are the church and the family. But sometimes the family should be coached as to how to support their children.

As for the invisible support system, St. Paul tells us about it in the epistle to the Hebrews, saying, "Therefore we also, since we are surrounded by so great a cloud of witnesses, let us lay aside every weight, and the sin which so easily ensnares us, and let us run with endurance the race that is set before us."[34] It is a race. I need endurance; I need to run. What will help me run with endurance the race that is set before me? First, of course, the grace of God, and second, the cloud of witnesses, since we are surrounded by so great a cloud of witnesses.

Make them choose a saint and develop a strong connection with this saint to help them overcome this sin. And ask this saint to be their intercessor. Of course, if they choose more than one saint, this will be beautiful: "Since we are surrounded by so great a cloud of witnesses, let us lay aside every weight, and the sin which so easily ensnares us." So, the support from the cloud of witnesses is needed to lay aside every weight and the sin which so easily ensnares us. Teach them about the intercession of the saints. Most of us who are orthodox believe in the intercession of the saints, but we do not apply it; we do not live it. Teach them how to convert this belief into practical experience.

---

34   Hebrews 12:1.

The Fourth Stage: Acting

If they are in the fourth stage, acting, we need to expect that some relapses will happen, because they are changing their comfort zone to a new comfort zone. Even in our sinfulness, this is our comfort zone. I am comfortable in my sinfulness. When I repent, I am trying to get out of this comfort zone into a new zone that is not comfortable for me right now. But I want this to be my new comfort zone. So in repentance, I am moving from this comfort zone to a new comfort zone.

So there is a tendency to relapse. Once the first relapse happens, Satan will tell them, "I told you, it is a hopeless case. Forget about it. Do not fight it anymore." That is what the devil will say. But I will not believe this. I need to keep pushing myself into the new comfort zone. So every time I relapse, again I will push myself through the grace of God and the intercession of the saints into the new comfort zone. Gradually, after some time, this will become my second nature and become who I am, and I will forget who I was. Explain this to them and support them, and give them encouragement even when they relapse.

Also, follow up with them. Sometimes they say, "I will do this and that," and we do not follow up with them, and they relapse and are embarrassed to come to us, and we do ask about them. Therefore, they lose hope, and nothing will happen. You need to know that these people have shame, are ashamed, and have low self-esteem. They are embarrassed, so we need to follow up with them. Do not wait until they come to us; we need to follow up with them. Also, discuss with them the challenges: Why did they relapse? Maybe because they were in the same environment, the same challenges with their parents or with their friends. What are the challenges that made them relapse?

The two important virtues they need in this stage are patience and forgiving oneself. I have heard it from many people who say, "I know God forgave me, but I cannot forgive myself." Forgiving oneself means accepting this gift of forgiveness from God, and to forgive myself, to be reconciled with myself, and to be patient. Those who endure to the end will be saved. This is what the Bible tells us: "He who endures to the end will be saved."[35] "By your patience possess your souls."[36] What does it mean to possess? It means your soul was lost. In order to get it back, to possess it again after it was lost, you can possess it only by patience. You need to teach them how to be patient with themselves and to accept their weaknesses, never to lose hope, and to trust in God.

The Fifth Stage: Perseverance

In the fifth stage, perseverance, there are definitely some victories they have achieved. Celebrate the victories in the Lord more than rebuking them for the

---

35   Matthew 10:22.
36   Luke 21:19.

relapses. For example, they will tell you, "I relapsed after five months. I felt I had recovered." So you can tell them, "Let us praise God for these five months, and as you were able to stay strong and victorious for five months, forget about the relapse; God will raise you again." Celebrate these victories in the Lord and tell them, "This relationship with God is the reason behind your victories."

And changing their soul or their mind from condemning and hating themselves, feeling that they are a failure, into thanksgiving and gratefulness will produce joy in their hearts. And this joy is their strength as we read in the Book of Nehemiah, "For the joy of the LORD is your strength."[37] In this stage, while we are celebrating the victories, we are bringing thanksgiving and gratefulness to the Lord in their hearts. And this will produce joy, and the joy will be their strength to completely overcome.

The Sixth Stage: Recovery

Their perseverance will lead to the last stage, which is recovery. Let me tell you, whether transgenderism or homosexuality, it is a struggle for the whole life, like any other sin. For example, if I am struggling with anger, it is the struggle of my whole life. But after having failed, now I am away from these thoughts after one year, two years, three years; I no longer feel that I am a woman trapped in a man's body.

---

37   Nehemiah 8:10.

59

Therefore, in this stage, besides thanksgiving to the Lord, I need watchfulness. Thanksgiving will keep me humble, that it is not through my power or my strength or my will, but it is through the grace of God. And humility is what protects me from relapsing or falling again. But what is important here is watchfulness. Sometimes when I get relaxed about the sin, Satan comes suddenly and attacks me. That is why I need to live the life of watchfulness. That is why the Bible says, "Watch and pray, lest you enter into temptation."[38] And with watchfulness comes prayer. As the Lord said, "Watch and pray." So they need humbleness, thanksgiving, watchfulness, and also joy in the Lord, as I explained before, for it gives them strength.

The last point in this stage is serving others when they are ready. Use them to serve other transgender persons. They will be the best to serve other transgender persons, but only when they are ready, when they are spiritually mature, when they have this strong relationship with God. Serving other transgender persons when they are recovered, they will fulfill their role in God. They are very helpful to others because they are an example of a successful story of recovery, and they understand the struggle.

Regardless of how much we say that we understand their struggle, in reality, we do not understand the struggle of homosexuality or transgenderism or a person going through divorce or whatever else, if I

---

38   Matthew 26:41.

have not gone through it myself. Yes, I try to empathize and understand with my mind and my spirit, and the grace of God will help us as clergy and servants to understand. But in the end, who will understand the mindset of an addict? It is the recovered addict. Who will understand the mindset of a transgender person? A recovered transgender person. So, using these people according to the calling of God, when they are ready, when they are spiritually mature to be able to serve, using these people to serve others will be very helpful.

Dealing with a Transgender Co-worker

There is one point with which I would like to conclude this chapter: How do we deal with a transgender person at work or in school or in the neighborhood, when they are not Christian, not interested in recovering? That is what they perceive as normal. You need to remember that your colleagues are made in God's image. And if they are transgender, they need prayers for God's grace to enlighten their minds. So we need to offer continual prayers for them.

And if there is an opportunity, if they come and ask you what you believe about this, you need, as Christians, to be able to speak the truth in love. As St. Paul told us, "Speaking the truth in love."[39] If they choose another name, it is okay to use this name, because many names can be used for a male and female; some names are common for males and

---

39   Ephesians 4:15.

females, and in different cultures, for example, Michel in the Egyptian culture is a male name, but here in the United States, Michelle is a female name. Even in the Egyptian culture, some names like Reda and Ismat can be used for males and females, and I am sure it is the same in American culture. If they choose a name, it is okay to use the name they give themselves.

But if they use the pronoun, I do not encourage you to use the wrong pronouns, because using the wrong pronouns is denying the truth. So, avoid using pronouns and instead use the new names. And we need to stand strong. If they push you to use the wrong pronouns, you need to speak out, but say the truth in love. And you can tell them that this is your freedom of speech, to speak out the truth. As you demand people to respect your beliefs, and I am calling you by the name you choose, again, you need to respect my beliefs, and do not pressure me to deny my beliefs, as I respect your beliefs. And do not be afraid to speak the truth in love, because the Holy Spirit is with you and will help you, and we need to be witnesses to our faith and the truth.

As I told you, the three things that we need to do with the people who are not willing or not interested are prayer, confronting them gently, speaking the truth in love, and not enabling them. Using the wrong pronoun is enabling them and not confronting them, nor addressing or saying the truth.

3

Dealing with Homosexuality

Not only does gender identity pertain to transgenderism, but also to homosexuality, because if I perceive myself as homosexual, then the expression of my sexuality is directed to the wrong gender. As I have previously said, God created us as male and female and compatible with each other, and sexual expression should be fulfilled through marriage. I would also like in these two chapters to address the issue of homosexuality. I will start by speaking about the reasons for homosexuality.

Reasons for Homosexuality

1. The Disruption of Early Family Relationships. If this relationship is affected, especially the relationship with the parent of the same gender, or if there is tension, this leads to psychological separation. This is why the child here identifies himself or herself more with the other gender, and as they grow, their gender begins to decrease. For example, a male child who is more associated with his mother would lose his masculinity, and because of this, he may choose either transgenderism or homosexuality. In adolescence, he would be attracted to discover the world of men if he were a boy, and sexual attraction to the same gender would happen due to the effect of hormonal changes during the time of puberty.

But not only is the relationship with the parent of the same gender a reason for homosexuality, but also the relationship with the parent of the other gender, like a son with his mother or a girl with her father, can lead to homosexuality or transgenderism. How can this be? For example, if a mother complains to her son about his father, about the problems she has with the father, her husband, she is unintentionally creating a psychological separation from his father. And the son, if he empathizes with the mother, might say, "I hate my father. Why are you staying with him? Go and divorce him." And the mother is sometimes happy that the children are taking her side. And many times they come to me and say, "Even my son tells me, 'Why are you staying with him, go and divorce him?'" Without realizing it, she is destroying the gender of her son by complaining to him about his father. This leads the son to identify with his mother, and he would gradually lose his masculinity and have a desire to explore the world of men in his adolescence. And so he would gradually be attracted to men, and with the hormones during puberty, it would be a sexual attraction. Or the opposite might happen, a father complaining to his daughter about her mother.

Another reason is the overprotection of a mother over her son. Because of this overprotection, she makes him so attached to her that he does not keep the balance between being attached to the father and the mother. And again, because he is overly attached to the mother, this creates psychological separation from the father. The mother here is not giving her son a chance to spend time with the father. That is why, in the first ten years, it is important to have father-son time, mother-daughter time, father-daughter time, and mother-son time, to ensure that the child builds a relationship with both parents equally.

It may also happen that a mother takes her son into the female world, and this can be applied to a father and his daughter as well. If she is attending a women's meeting, she takes her son. If there is an activity for women in church or society, she takes her son with her, because he is just a little boy. In some churches, they separate boys and girls even in the primary school classes of Sunday school, and because she has, for example, two girls and one boy, she would send the son with the two girls into their Sunday school class for girls. Therefore, he is more involved in the female world, which decreases his masculinity. Or it might happen that the gender of the child was belittled. This happens more with girls than boys, making fun of her because she is a girl, making fun of the female gender in general. So, the effect of the disruption of early family relationships in general is a main reason for homosexuality.

2. The Effect of Trauma. Usually, when a person is traumatized, they want to get some pleasure or happiness, and the easiest coping mechanism for pleasure is derived from sexual experiences. Even the people who had fallen into masturbation and quit it for a very long time, when something happens to them, someone bothers them or makes them feel down, they want some pleasure, so they relapse and fall again into masturbation. I am not saying that this is a correct coping mechanism, but I am saying the easiest coping mechanism to get pleasure is derived from sexual experiences, either from masturbation or experiencing homosexual activity with ungodly friends. It can happen at school, and it can happen with ungodly friends of the family or relatives. And then, the child will have mixed feelings or mixed messages, the feelings of guilt and pleasure at the same time. He likes the pleasure, but he feels guilty about what happened. And this leads to confusion and lasts with him even after adolescence. And gradually, he will suppress the guilt because he wants the pleasure; so he suppresses the guilt yet keeps the pleasure.

3. The Effect of Society. Between the ages of 5 and 12 years, females and males like to play with the same gender, although it may be now between 5 and 10 years. At the age of 10 or 12, opposite gender attraction begins, and this is normal. In this stage, from 5-10 or 5-12, if the male is not strong in his masculinity and begins to be bullied by his male peers, this will lead him to choose female friends as his comfort zone. Although the norm in this age is to be attracted to the same gender, now because he is bullied by the males, he will have female friends. So when adolescence comes, he wants to discover the world of men, because he did not discover it during the ages of 5-12. And with adolescence and puberty, there are also the hormones, so sexual desire. Therefore, this creates in him same-sex attraction. He wants to be attracted to the same sex, so he can understand it.

4. The Effect of the Homosexual Society. We do not want to deny the effect of the homosexual society, which normalizes homosexuality as an alternative lifestyle. Out of curiosity, he wants to experience this world and continue in it just out of curiosity, nothing more. Some youth said to me, "We are starting to watch homosexual pornography, to know how these people get pleasure from sexual activity."

5. The Effect of Addiction and Habituation. Let me assume that there is a predisposition to homosexuality because of one of the aforementioned reasons: relationship with parents, effect of homosexual society, and so on. There is already, therefore, a predisposition toward homosexuality. Then they experience homosexuality even once and feel pleasure, because there is pleasure in any sexual sin. This pleasurable experience, with the predisposition toward homosexuality and the positive homosexual thoughts from society, will lead to more homosexual experiences, and they might end up identifying themselves as homosexual or transgender.

The last point I would like to make is that, as the homosexual desires begin to grow in the person, the person has a choice to act on them or fight them. When some people ask me if homosexuality is a choice, I say to them that it is not necessarily so. Many people, because of trauma or abuse, did not choose to be homosexual. Therefore, it is not necessarily a choice, but it is their choice whether to act on it or to fight it. This is the choice: to accept it or to reject it. For example, sometimes you have a reason to be angry, but you also have a choice whether to follow your anger or to manage it and control it. So what are some guidelines for recovery from homosexuality, and these can also be applied to transgenderism?

Motives for Recovery from Homosexuality and Transgenderism

1. Faith and Religion. We need to ask ourselves: What are the motives for change? Why would a person who is getting pleasure from homosexuality consider change? Faith and religion. When they know that it is a sin, and the Bible says that no homosexuals can inherit the Kingdom of God,[40] this in itself can be a motive for change.

2. The Psychological Struggle. Another motive to change is the psychological struggle. Many people suffer from stress and anxiety, and many people, unfortunately,

---

40   See 1 Corinthians 6:9.

reach the stage of committing suicide. And the argument of homosexuals here is that homosexuals commit suicide not because of homosexuality but because of the rejection by the community or society. They say that if society had not rejected them, they would not have committed suicide. But again, this is not true, for at least two reasons. The first reason is that, in many countries all over the world, they now have their rights, and there are laws supporting them, and there are national days in the country to celebrate LGBTQ, yet the percentage of suicide among homosexuals is still increasing. I cannot connect this and that.

The second reason is as follows. Let us ask ourselves, what is the percentage of suicide among other minorities or other groups that are rejected or treated as second-class? For example, persecuted Christians. If it is true that the feeling of rejection by society is the reason for the increase in suicide, then persecuted Christians would commit suicide. They are not only rejected but also persecuted. They are killed, kidnapped, their churches are burned, and so on. But we never heard of Christians committing suicide because of rejection or because of persecution. Not only have we never heard that, but we see rather that they become stronger. So the idea that being rejected is causing homosexuals to commit suicide is untrue.

3. The Desire to Have a Normal Family. When homosexuals marry, they marry homosexuals, so they will never have a normal family. They will never have children of their own. And also, the transgender person, if he is a male and has become a female, whom will he marry? If he marries a male, most of the males will not accept to marry a transgender female. So he will end up marrying a transgender person like him or a homosexual. These two types of marriage are not normal, because if he marries another transgender, both of their genitalia and manhood or womanhood are destroyed, so they will not have a normal family. And if he marries a homosexual, meaning, he is male and he made himself female and he married another female, again, they cannot have children or a normal family. I do not think a straight male or female would be interested in marrying a transgender person, because these people would want to have a normal family. So the desire to have a normal family can also be a motive for recovery.

Recovery from Homosexuality

Let me, however, define what recovery is. Recovery is not merely stopping or quitting, but rather recovery is a personality development in which the person does not have the attraction. If a homosexual stops practicing homosexuality completely and quits completely, but they still have an attraction toward homosexuals, we can say that they are on the road to recovery. Yes, they are struggling, and this struggle is accepted before God if they are fighting the good fight. But to say that they are recovered completely, this has to happen when they do not have an attraction toward the same sex anymore.

Goals of Recovery

That is why when we speak about the goals of recovery, there are three goals of recovery: behavior, feeling, and personality change. The first goal has to do with behavior, to reach a stable quitting for a long time from these practices, and to establish a satisfying heterosexual life. Feeling means to decrease the same-sex attraction. So this same-sex attraction decreases until it ends, and the heterosexual attraction increases. As for personality development, in their minds, they are heterosexual and cannot call themselves homosexual.

Overcoming Any Barriers in the Relationship with the Opposite Gender

When a man is homosexual, there are barriers in the relationship with females. But now, he can overcome any barrier in the relationship with the other gender. The question here is whether or not all homosexuals have decreased masculinity, because earlier I said that there is a decrease in masculinity, so he is attracted to discover the world of men. But does this imply that all homosexuals have weak masculinity? No, many homosexuals have a strong masculinity, not a weak one. But what is the issue here for these homosexuals? The issue here is that there is a barrier to dealing with the other gender. They have a barrier to connecting and being attracted to the other gender.

Treatment of Homosexuality

When we speak about treatment, there are three aspects working together at the same time. The first aspect is connecting with oneself; the second aspect is quitting, how to completely quit any homosexual activity; and the third aspect is connecting with others, especially with the other gender. So when you counsel a homosexual, you need to work on these three areas. To connect with oneself, to connect with others, especially the other gender, and to completely quit homosexual activity. Let me speak a little about each of these three aspects.

1. Connecting with Oneself

The goal of this is that the person reaches a level of maturity and develops life skills. I just want to say that these three aspects are not three stages, in that a person would have to finish this stage and move to the second stage, and then the third stage. But rather, the three work together at the same time. So what do I mean by connecting with oneself?

1. Knowing My Feelings and Expressing Them. I need to know my feelings and express them, whether they are right or wrong, because my feelings are my feelings. I need to learn how to connect with them and express them.

2. Understanding My Feelings. Not only do I need to be able to express my feelings, but also to understand them. Understanding them means discovering the contributing factors that make one identify as homosexual. So I should know the reason behind saying that I am a homosexual. Is it out of curiosity, or peer pressure, or was I bullied when I was young? Did I have a wrong relationship with my parents? Is it trauma?

3. Understanding My Feelings Toward the Partner. Also, understanding one's feelings toward their homosexual partner, if they are in an active relationship. So part of connecting with myself is understanding my feelings toward the homosexual partner, how one perceives their partner? Is he dependent on him? Is there a feeling of dependency in my pleasure, in my satisfaction, in my being content?

Also, am I looking for love and care from the partner that I missed from my parents? I have heard this from many youths. They say, "He loves me and cares for me. My father does not care about me as he cares about me." So this is a contributing factor: to find a person who loves you and cares for you. Also, am I, in my mind, replacing the parent with the partner? So in my mind, because I am looking for a mother figure or a father figure, I am replacing this father or mother with the partner.

And the best approach is to ask them to write down their feelings and to understand themselves. In connecting with myself, the first thing is to know my feelings and express them; the second thing is to understand my feelings, and then to understand my feelings toward the partner.

We need to understand what affects what. Do my feelings affect my mind, or do my mind or my thoughts affect my feelings? Thoughts affect the feelings, not the opposite. And this is the beauty of the verse in the epistle to the Romans that says, "Be transformed by the renewing of your mind."[41] So if I change my thoughts, if I renew my thoughts, then the feelings will change, not the opposite.

And there are some verses which are very difficult to apply if you do not understand this principle, that thoughts affect the feelings and not the opposite, for example, "Love your enemies."[42] How can you love your enemies? This is especially the case if you are speaking here about love in terms of emotions. How can I develop feelings and emotions toward my enemy who hurts me and wants to destroy me? So "love your enemies" starts as a decision, a choice I make, not just a feeling. There is no button to push that can change your feelings to love them. But I can decide to do the works of love toward my enemy even if I do not have the feeling. As St. Paul said, "If your enemy is hungry, feed him; if he is thirsty, give him a drink."[43] So when I make this decision and start doing the works of love toward my enemy, love will be processed by the grace of God from here to there, and my heart and my feelings will change.

---

41   Romans 12:2.

42   Matthew 5:44.

43   Romans 12:20.

This can happen even between couples. When a husband or a wife says, "I hate my spouse, I cannot endure him [or her] anymore, I want to just get divorced." If they made a decision to love them and do the works of love toward them, the feelings of love will gradually return to them. And this is the principle upon which the movie Fireproof is built. This movie is a good movie; you should watch it. How do you make your marriage fireproof? This is the idea of the movie. And even if you hate your spouse, just do the works of love and keep doing them. Two things will happen: gradually, your heart will be changed as the Bible tells us, "Be transformed by the renewing of your mind"; and the second thing is that if you are sowing love, you will reap love, so gradually your spouse will be changed.

4. Observing My Thoughts and Beliefs. After understanding my feelings and understanding the feelings toward my partner, I need to observe my thoughts and beliefs, because there are some wrong thoughts and beliefs that contributed to the feeling that I am transgender or homosexual. And the culture that is around us plants these thoughts and wrong principles in our minds.

Write your thoughts down. And after you write all these thoughts down, then in another column, write alternative thoughts or correct thoughts or Biblical thoughts or renewed thoughts. In front of every thought that is contributing to homosexuality, write the correct thought and try to adapt and accept these correct belief systems; and this is the renewal of your mind. The renewal of the mind in Greek means *metanoia*: the word *nous* means mind. *Metanoia* is translated to repentance; so, repentance starts here. I write down my wrong belief system and correct it based on the authority of the Scripture. I pray about it, and I ask God to help me and to renew my thoughts.

This principle is very important in our lives, not only in treating transgenderism or homosexuality, but in our lives in general. Your thoughts determine your feelings, and both of them determine your actions. Anger, for example, in order to manage it and control it, you need to first renew your thoughts and feelings, and then you will be able to manage your anger. One of the wrong thoughts is saying, "My children trigger or frustrate me. I get angry because of them." The reality is that it is not your children who trigger you, but your lack of endurance and patience, and not understanding childhood; these are what make you angry. Let me prove it to you right now.

If there was a gathering of 25 persons, and somebody came in and cursed all of them—here the action is the same for all of them—are all going to have the same reaction? No. Why? Because each one of them will interpret this action differently, and based on how they interpret this action, then they develop a feeling, either frustration or even compassion for him, because he is breaking the commandment of God. And both your thoughts and your feelings determine your reaction. So your reaction is not a reaction to the action of the other person, but your reaction is always a reaction to your interpretation of the other's behavior. That is the renewal of the mind that St. Paul spoke about. If I start to think differently, to think in a way to develop positive feelings instead of negative feelings, then both of them will help me to rejoice in the Lord and to manage my anger.

When St. Paul was in prison, some people became very active in ministry. You can read this in the first chapter of the epistle to the Philippians. They became very active in ministry to add pain and suffering to St. Paul, as if they were telling him, "You are in prison, and we took your place. Your children are now our children; you cannot communicate with them, and we are taking them as our children." St. Paul said, "The former preach Christ from selfish ambition, not sincerely, supposing to add affliction to my chains."[44] But St. Paul started to interpret their actions differently. If he had looked at it in a way that they were adding more pain to him and wanted to frustrate him, he would have been very angry at them. But how did he start to look at it differently? He said, "Only that in every way, whether in pretense or truth, Christ is preached; and in this I rejoice, yes, and will rejoice."[45] Whether for a good or a bad reason, the name of Christ is preached; and I am happy because the name of Christ is preached, so I rejoice. This shows you how

44   Philippians 1:16.
45   Philippians 1:18.

the renewal of the mind—how to think differently—will not make you angry or upset or disappointed; rather, the opposite can happen, and you will rejoice.

Back to homosexuality and transgenderism, when I start renewing my mind and think differently, by correcting all the wrong beliefs and thoughts, then the way I perceive myself will be changed. I am no longer going to perceive myself as homosexual or transgender. We are still speaking about knowing and expressing oneself. Thus far, we spoke about, first, knowing my feelings and expressing them; second, understanding my feelings; third, understanding the feelings toward the partner; fourth, examining my thoughts and correcting my beliefs.

5. Accepting Myself and Not Accepting How I Identify Myself. There is a difference between accepting the person and accepting the sin. Many of them deal with guilt and shame, and they feel defeated, and they hate themselves, so they need to deal with guilt and shame. Some may be shunned by society, church, and family; and they feel rejected. So we, as servants or counselors, should help them accept themselves even if they are rejected by others around them.

If they are walking in the path of repentance and start the journey, and they know that it is a sin and that they are still struggling with it but have not overcome it, they need to understand that God loves them and accepts their repentance and struggle, even if they have not yet defeated the sin. Even before they start the path of repentance, God still loves them, and if God is punishing or disciplining any one of them, this is so that He may lead them back to the path of repentance.

Many of them tend not to forgive themselves, and this leads to depression. And with this depression, they want some pleasure, so they will go to the coping mechanism of sexual sins and the pleasure of sexual sins, and the vicious cycle begins again. That is why accepting oneself and forgiving oneself are very important.

6. Knowing My Needs and Fulfilling Them in a Non-sexual Way. Being transgender or being homosexual means that they have some needs, and in a way, they satisfy these needs by saying that they are transgender or homosexual. So they need to know their needs, write them down, and know how to fulfill them in a non-sexual way. They should write down their needs for their homosexual partner, and they need to begin fulfilling them in a healthy and non-sexual way with the help of the clergy or a servant or a therapist. For example, if they have a need for love or care, how can they satisfy this need away from a homosexual partner?

7. Improving My Relationship with My Body. Due to homosexual acts, they might have a lot of physical diseases, so they need to get treated for these diseases, and they need to love and respect their body and understand that it is the temple of the Holy Spirit.

8. Addressing Past Trauma or Abuse. If there are old wounds, for example, if they were exposed to trauma or abuse, they need to address the trauma or abuse. And one of the very effective ways to address them is by asking them to write letters to the abuser. And I have tried this method with many people, and it helped them. They should write a letter directed to the abuser in the second person, not as a journal. In a journal, they would say, "He did this to me." But in the second person, they would say, "You did this to me. Why did you do this to me?" They should put all their feelings down with honesty, but without sin, as the Bible tells us, "Be angry, and do not sin."[46] So they can express their frustration, their disappointment, even their anger, but in a Christian way.

And then after they write the letter, they have three options: they can shred it and throw it away; or they can share it with a trusted person like a father of confession or a trusted servant or a counselor; or they can send it to the abuser. Regardless of whether they shred it, or share it with somebody else, or send it to the abuser, it will have the same effect in the end, because the purpose of this is not confrontation; rather, the purpose of it is externalization. I have this anger inside me toward what happened, so externalizing it is part of the healing. This is why I told you that it should not be written as a journal, but it should be written in the second person as a letter directed to a person. I am externalizing it in a

---

46   Ephesians 4:26.

very physical way by writing it. It is as if I took this anger and frustration inside me and put it outside me. This is part of the healing. And of course, this healed many people, besides prayer, returning to God, asking for healing from God, and so on. So this is not the only thing to do. And as I told you, I tried this with many people, and after writing the letter, they felt at peace.

Sometimes we do this, but not in this way. For example, by daydreaming, you make a scenario in your mind that he comes to you, and you respond to him in this way. This is a type of externalization, and it gives some peace. But when you write it down, you are totally externalizing it by putting it down on a piece of paper, but in a Christian way. Satan cannot cast out Satan. If you are externalizing it in a non-Christian way, it will not help you.

9. Having a Strong Spiritual Canon and Connection with the Sacraments. As I told you, healing comes from God. "I am the LORD who heals you."[47] And without having this connection with the Lord, it will be difficult for a person to be healed. I told you there are three aspects in therapy. The first aspect is connecting with oneself, and under this, I mentioned nine points. The second one is quitting. Quitting what?

---

47   Exodus 15:26.

2. Quitting

The goal here is to break bad habits and to redirect the sexual energy in the right direction.

1. Completely Stopping All Sexual Acts. They need to completely stop all sexual acts by removing all the triggers and by building a healthy atmosphere. Yes, it is sometimes addictive. These sins are addictive, and because there is pleasure, these sins are beloved. Sometimes they do not want to lose the pleasure, which is why they are not willing to quit these sins. If there is poison in the honey, I will not eat it, because I know that in the end it will kill me. So again, I should not let the pleasure change my thoughts, but rather the opposite, my thoughts should overcome the pleasure. Completely stop all sexual acts.

2. Completely Ending Any Relationship with Any Homosexual. This is especially the case with those who perceive it as an alternative lifestyle. So even if they have friends who are homosexual, they need to end these relationships completely, because bad company corrupts good habits; these are not partners but just friends, but they believe that homosexuality is an alternative lifestyle. We call this principle radical amputation. The Lord said, "If your right eye causes you to sin, pluck it out and cast it from you."[48] If your eye causes you to sin, did he say, "Close it"? No, He said, "pluck it out." When He said, "If your right hand causes you to sin," did He say, "Withdraw it"? No,

---

48   Matthew 5:29.

He said, "Cut it off and cast it from you."[49] Radical amputation. So here they need to end any relationship with any homosexual.

3. Ending All Romantic and Dependent Relationships. The second point was about ending a relationship, even with those who are not partners, like a friendship or companionship. The third point is about ending all romantic and dependent relationships, not only with people but also with the triggers.

Places. For example, they need to write down the places that they went to together, because going back to these places, even alone, will make them fall into temptation. So they need to write these places down and avoid them in order to avoid these triggers.

People. Also, they need to write down the people to whom they are attracted, whether they are practicing with them or not, and definitely the people with whom they practiced homosexuality. They need to avoid them completely, both the places where they went with them, and the people they are attracted to, regardless of whether they practiced with them or not.

Challenges of Staying Away from Them. They need to write down the challenges of staying away from them, to acknowledge these challenges, and to deal with them. And maybe you can ask for guidance from a priest or a counselor. It is difficult to avoid these people with whom they have had a romantic relationship, so how can they overcome this?

49   Matthew 5:30.

4. Reasons for Needing These People. They need to write down reasons why they need this person, because understanding why they need this person will help them to stay away from the person. And as a counselor, or as clergy, we should understand and share this with them, that it is painful to cut the sources off, to cut all these relationships off. Although they are sinful relationships, to cut them off or end them is painful. I should not say something like, "I am surprised by how you cannot end this relationship." There is no compassion here in a statement like this; there is no understanding here. But saying it differently, like, "I understand that ending this relationship is painful and hard, and that it is not easy. I understand this, because I can see clearly there are certain needs which are fulfilled through this relationship, but we trust in God, as St. Paul said, 'I can do all things through Christ who strengthens me.'[50] I trust that God will comfort you and He will give you His peace that surpasses all understanding."

So it is important that you be understanding and share with them that, yes, you know it is painful and it is not an easy thing to do. Some youth say, "I went to speak with the priest, and he does not understand me." Yes, that is why they will not obey, not because they are rebellious persons, but because they feel that you do not understand them. So, showing understanding is very important, although understanding does not mean agreeing. I understand why a thief stole money,

---

50   Philippians 4:13.

but I do not agree with this. I understand why David committed adultery and murder, but I do not agree with this.

5. The Impact of Social Media on Me. Maybe during this time, when they are trying to quit, they have to completely cut off social media. And cut off pornography and masturbation completely.

6. Understanding My Triggers. What are the triggers that make them fall again into these bad habits? For example, if they decided to call their partner again, to visit or invite him or her over. What is the trigger? What are the needs at this time that made them do this? Most probably, it is a need for pleasure. And by the way, these people do not love the other person, but they love the pleasure that they get from this relationship. Like the addict, he does not love heroin, but he loves the feeling he gets when he is abusing heroin. They might say, "I love him." But no, they do not. Because if I love a person, I need to walk with him in the way of repentance. But here, they do not love the other person; they love the feeling, the pleasure they get from the relationship with the other person.

3. Connecting with Others

As we said, in recovery or treatment, first, connect with oneself, and second, quit. The third aspect is connecting with others. The goal of this step is to develop a healthy and true gender identity.

1. Building Healthy Relationships with the Same Gender. They need to build healthy relationships with the same gender. The definition of healthy is three things: non-romantic, non-sexual, and non-dependent. It is non-romantic, that is, not a romantic love. Non-sexual, that is, there is no sexual activity at all, neither hugging nor complete sexual activity. And non-dependent, that is, they should not be dependent on the person to satisfy their needs for love or care or pleasure or anything else. So when I say healthy boundaries, these are non-romantic, non-sexual, and non-dependent. So learn how to have a healthy relationship with the same gender. But this will happen hand-in-hand when you reconcile with yourself. That is why I mentioned connecting with oneself and quitting, before this one, although I said that the three go together at the same time.

And they also need to reconcile with family members who hurt them. When I choose to be transgender or homosexual, I hurt my family, and my family goes through pain. So part of their recovery is to reconcile with their family members, because sometimes, their look, their pain, their suffering can trigger in them the guilt, the shame, the depression; and the solution is to ask the family members to accept them, because if they had accepted my sin, they would have enabled me the wrong way. And again, if they go through depression, they enter this vicious cycle, because I want to please myself, and the easiest way to please myself is through sexual desire. So I go into this cycle.

2. Building Healthy Relationships with the Other Gender. Homosexuals develop barriers to dealing with the other gender. They are not comfortable with that, and so is the case for transgender people also. So they need to learn how to develop a relationship with the opposite gender. These relationships are not for marriage—they are not getting to know girls because they are now thinking of marriage, but rather so that they may learn how to deal with the other gender properly.

3. Learning How Not to be Dependent on Others. They need to learn how not to depend on others to meet their needs. They should not be dependent. How can they fulfill their needs? First, to fulfill their needs, they need to learn how to depend on God, on themselves, and on a group of friends, not on one friend only. By the way, there is nothing called independence. In relationships, it is called interdependence: I depend on you, and you depend on me. When I depend on one person, we call this a wrong dependent relationship. I get all my needs fulfilled through this person. That is why I said that they need to learn how to depend on God, on themselves, and on a group of friends, not on one person.

That is why they need to be part of a godly and spiritual community like the church, because in this godly and spiritual community, they will learn how to depend on God, on others, and on themselves; for example, being active in a youth meeting in church.

Also, people in the community around a repentant homosexual or transgender person need to learn how to provide a loving and accepting atmosphere for this repentant. As St. Paul said to the people in Corinth, "You ought rather to forgive and comfort him, lest perhaps such a one be swallowed up with too much sorrow. Therefore I urge you to reaffirm your love to him."[51] We, as clergy and servants, need to ask the people around this repentant homosexual or transgender person to reaffirm their love toward them.

Recovering homosexuals also need to develop healthy communication skills. How to communicate with the same gender and the opposite gender, maturely and purely. One of the things that helps is being involved in sports and exercise. And they need to learn the difference between love and lust. Lust is seeking my own pleasure. So I say, "I love this person." There is a difference between saying, "I love this food," and "I love this person." I love this food because when I eat it, it gives me pleasure; this is what we call eros. But Christian love is sacrificial love; it is love that leads toward salvation, not toward sin.

Recovered Homosexuals and Marriage

When will a recovered homosexual person be ready for marriage? When can I encourage them to get married?

1. When they have stopped all sexual activity for at least one year.

---

51   2 Corinthians 2:7–8.

2. When the attraction toward the opposite gender starts to grow.

3. I should warn them that recovery is not a one-step process; it is a life journey. So even if they stopped for five years, they should remain watchful because there can be a relapse at any moment.

4

Prevention & Awareness

As I said in the first chapter, sometimes we are reactive, not proactive. That is why we need to teach clearly about homosexuality from a very young age, but again with age-appropriate topics. What are the topics that are appropriate for a young age? And as I said before, simply saying that God created a male and a female, and that marriage is between a male and a female. We can teach them something like saying that no two males can make a family, no two females can make a family. This is a lesson about homosexuality for three- or four-year-old children. Marriage is between a male and a female. I think our Sunday school curriculums and our preaching in general avoid addressing these issues. I do not know the reason, but perhaps we are afraid of the community.

We have some questions for the Church servants and pre-servants, which they have to answer every year, to make sure they have the right doctrines, the right understanding of the Scripture, and the right moral code. And in this questionnaire, two or three questions are about homosexuality. The answers to these questions are confidential and not shared with anybody, except perhaps with only the priest and the Sunday school coordinators. What I am about to say is a fact. Some servants came to us and refused to answer these questions, although they told us that, yes, they know it is a sin, but they would not write it on paper, because perhaps they would lose their job because of this. And although we told them that it was confidential, they still refused to put it on paper. Unfortunately, some of us are still afraid and are not courageous enough, or we are not willing to take the risk of even losing our jobs to defend the truth. Our fathers, the martyrs, did not lose their jobs but lost their lives to defend the truth.

What I am trying to say is that we need to teach about homosexuality; we need to teach about transgenderism. We need to teach what sexuality is in the economy of God and to teach families the reasons for homosexuality and how to avoid them. What is the correct parenting approach? I mentioned many examples of parenting mistakes. So we need to teach and coach the parents about how to raise their children in the correct way. Also, we need to teach parents and servants about the early signs of homosexuality, to be able to identify these signs and deal with it early, not to wait until it becomes an advanced case.

Also, in teaching about homosexuality, we need to teach about the hope of recovery, because most of the world says that you cannot convert somebody who is homosexual to be heterosexual; but, no, there are successful cases of recovery. Maybe you should know that conversion therapy, which is a therapy to change a homosexual to heterosexual, is illegal in 37 states in America.

And since I mentioned conversion therapy, there are two types of conversion therapy: secular therapy and Christian therapy. The secular depends mainly on changing the external, not changing the heart. But the Christian conversion therapy starts by changing the heart, and then the outside will be changed.

Also, we need to coach parents how a father should take his son into the world of men and how a mother should take her daughter into the world of women, and how it is not proper to treat your son as a female and vice versa, and we need to teach parents how to make their children proud of and thankful for their gender.

If a parent comes to me and says that their son or daughter is homosexual or transgender, how should we advise them? First, you need to show understanding and empathy to the parent. Believe me, it is very hurtful to the parents that a son or a daughter is transgender or homosexual, so you need to support them, even if they are the reason in one way or another, even if they are violent or discriminatory against a certain gender.

It is not the right time now to rebuke them or tell them, "Yes, it is because of your parenting style." It is not the time to say this. But listen and understand the possible reasons. Take a history before jumping to conclusions or speaking of recovery or giving them solutions; listen and understand the possible reasons. In the Book of Proverbs, it says, "He who answers a matter before he hears it, it is folly and shame to him."[52] If you answer something before you listen to it and understand it, it is shameful. So listen carefully, do not jump to conclusions. Try to figure out where the son or daughter is on the ladder of change, on which one of the six stages of change.

You need to give support to the family and restructure the family to be a healthy, godly, and functional family. It is called structural family therapy, how to restructure the family to set the hierarchy correctly and to correct the relationship and the communication between parents and children. And discuss the reasons with the parents without blaming, and try to build a relationship between the parents and the children. Explain to them their role in the support system without enabling, and how to support their son or daughter without enabling him or her.

One of the common mistakes I noticed is that one parent accepts and supports, while the other parent completely rejects and attacks. And when I said one parent accepts and supports, not only accepting the

---

52   Proverbs 18:13.

person but also the sin. Both parents should follow the Word of God. You cannot have one parent accepting the sin and accepting the son or daughter under the guise of love. This will make the other parent very angry with the spouse and with the son or daughter. This will never heal the situation. So both of them should agree to follow the Word of God. And when they agree together on how to handle the situation, this is in the best interest of their son or daughter.

How Should Servants and Clergy Deal with Homosexuals?

1. We need to agree and follow the Biblical teaching that homosexuality is a sin. Transgenderism is a sin. And this should be clear in our teachings, because some clergy and some servants, to be politically correct, deny the sinful nature of homosexuality and transgenderism, and just say that it is an illness. No, it is not only an illness. If I am disordering the economy of God, then it is a sin. And as the verse from Deuteronomy says, "It is an abomination to the Lord."[53]

2. Yes, we understand that people may not choose to be homosexual or transgender, but they still have the choice to fight it or live with it. Yes, not every homosexual or transgender person makes a decision to be this way. There are many cases where it is not their choice.

---

53   Deuteronomy 22:5.

3. We need to understand that some cases are due to personality or mental disorders. And these cases have to be treated professionally first. Yes, it is a sin. For example, a child has a mental disability, and so he may curse and steal. I cannot say that stealing and cursing are not sins. These are sins. But how God will hold him accountable for this is a different story. Yes, these are sinful behaviors, but maybe God will not hold them accountable for these sins because of their mental illness. But this does not make it not a sin. If there is a mental illness or personality disorder, this has to be addressed and treated. And we need to direct the parents that their child needs professional help.

And we need to differentiate between a person who believes that it is a sin but is not willing to change, and a person who believes that it is a sin and is willing to change and repent, and a person who does not believe that it is a sin. There are three categories here.

We need to exclude the people who refuse to believe that it is a sin, because they will have a negative influence on our children, and this is very clear in the first epistle to the Corinthians. St. Paul said that we should exclude these people. "Put away from yourselves the evil person."[54] What makes this person evil? They are making what is wrong right, what is evil good. That is the definition of an evil person. If this is a person's belief, then they will spread

---

54   1 Corinthians 5:13.

this among the youth and will have a negative effect on them. If they believe it is a sin, but is unwilling to change, then, as I said in the six stages, I need to follow all the steps or aspects, first understanding why they are unwilling, and start the therapeutic ladder, step by step. If they believe it is a sin and are willing to change, this will be easier to walk with them on the journey of recovery.

What do I do if at my work or my school they are imposing certain values on me that I have to follow? Thank God that until now the Constitution has not changed. You have constitutional rights, so do not be afraid to use your constitutional rights, that no one should impose on you certain values that you do not believe in. It is your constitutional right. Also, explain what you can do and what you cannot do, and demand respect for your beliefs and your rights. This is protected by the Constitution, and if you need to seek legal advice, please do.

4. You need to be willing to take the risk of losing some privileges and some rights for the sake of the truth if you defend the truth. Our fathers, the martyrs, lost their lives. Be assured, as St. Paul said, "For whom I have suffered the loss of all things, and count them as rubbish, that I may gain Christ and be found in Him."[55]

---

55 Philippians 3:8–9.

The Problem of Homosexuality and Transgenderism

There is a long-term problem here and now. Here and now is what we are talking about—that is, the present. But what do I mean by a long-term problem? We need to focus on how to solve the long-term problem. We need to raise the people's awareness regarding the media and social media, because they are strong promoters of homosexuality and transgenderism. In the election and voting, no party will fully defend the economy of God, but at least we need to vote for the party that will defend the moral and Biblical standards, to protect our children. Our homes should be very watchful and spiritual.

Schools are now a challenge. That is why we are now encouraging virtual schools, Coptic schools, and homeschooling. I believe that now you need to think and choose schools, because many private schools and public schools are also promoting homosexuality and transgenderism. So you need to think about which schools you will enroll your children in. Teach the parents in your church about this, so they will be careful when they apply for schools for their children. I will try to answer some questions that came to me regarding homosexuality. As servants and parents, I am sure you will be confronted with these questions.

Questions & Answers on Homosexuality

Did God create us this way?

What is the reference for this question? What is my reference that I will rely on in answering this question? Am I going to rely on research? What is the credibility of medical and scientific research, as I spoke before? According to a paper published by Cambridge University explaining why so much scientific research is likely to be false, the main reason is publication bias. What is your reference to the question of whether God created us homosexual or transgender, or not? The authority, the infallibility, and the inspiration of the Word of God should be our reference.

There are very interesting studies called the twin studies. If homosexuality is genetic, then the concordance rate should be 100% in identical twins. You know that the twins can be identical or non-identical. Therefore, if it is genetic, then both identical twins should be homosexual. But according to a study done by Bailey and Pillard (1991), a genetic study of male sexual orientation, they found that, of the homosexuals they studied, only 50% of identical twins were both homosexual, not because of genetics, but because of similar environmental, familial, and societal influences. Thus, according to this study, it was decided that there is no genetic determination. A later study done by King and McDonald (1992), published in the British Journal of Psychiatry, concerning homosexuals who are twins, stated that the rate is only 25%, not even 50%, so there is no genetic determination. If there were a genetic determination, then both of the identical twins would be homosexual.

What about the "gay gene"?

There was a study done by Hamer (1993) in which he mentioned that he believed that he had discovered the gay gene on the X chromosome, Xq28. But in a later study done by researcher Benjamin Neale, a geneticist who is co-director of the Stanley Center for Psychiatric Research and is a member at the Broad Institute of MIT and Harvard, he said in a research article in the Journal of Science (2019), "There is certainly no single genetic determinant (sometimes referred to as the 'gay gene' in the media)." So he said that it is impossible to predict their behavior just from their genome. I am trying to give you the names of these studies because all these studies are available, public information. Later on, Michael Bronski, Professor of the Practice in Media and Activism in Studies of Women, Gender, and Sexuality, and he is the author of *A Queer History of the United States*, said, "Why is this even a question? And why are you doing this research? The genetic part of it, even if there are things people can discover, seems to me to be a minute aspect of the complexity of how people are sexual... It seems to me like doing an analysis of a great novel like *Anna*

Karenina and focusing on the commas and periods rather than the themes." In this great novel, you are focusing on the comma, not on the themes. There is no genetic determination, so the idea that we are born this way is not true.

And just for the sake of discussion, let me say we are born this way, and there is genetic determination. But this does not make it normal. If a person is born with congenital heart disease or Down Syndrome, does this make Down Syndrome normal? So even if it is genetic, this does not make it normal or an alternative lifestyle. It must be treated and labeled as wrong.

What is the appropriate age to start introducing this issue, and how can it be introduced at home? How can we make sure we are telling them the right thing and not exposing them to something they are not aware of?

To answer this question, give them a simple explanation of marriage between Adam and Eve. So, just a simple explanation, marriage happens between a male and a female. Make them proud of their gender. Take the boy into the world of boys and the girl into the world of girls. Plant in their minds who is the final judge when there are contradictory opinions. Plant in their minds the truth when there are contradictory opinions. And make sure to fulfill their needs for love, care, and healthy connections with their parents.

Why is homosexuality on the rise within the Coptic community? Is this due to social influence and media? And what resources can help us?

There are many reasons why there is a rise within our Coptic community, like its legalization, people who push for tolerance, social media influence, media and brainwashing of our young children, social trends, schools and education, and poor parenting. All these factors together contribute to the rise of same-sex attraction.

If I think that my teen may be attracted to the same sex, how should I talk to him about it? He mentioned the subject several times, so I am getting concerned.

You need to build a strong bond of Christian love with your son or daughter. Show him the importance of a strong spiritual life. Have an open and honest discussion about his beliefs on homosexuality. Ask him questions like, "What would you do if Satan tempted you to try this experience?" Agree on the reference; this is very important. What is your reference to say that homosexuality is right or wrong? What is your reference? What authority? Is the authority science or research or medicine or reason or your feelings? Or is the authority the word of God? What is his reference, and based on this reference, we need to correct the wrong beliefs. It is important to expose the thoughts and warfare in the very early stages. Our early Church Fathers taught us the importance of exposing our thoughts, and this is important in confession. When I expose my thoughts in confession, my father of confession can weaken their influence over me. Explain the hope of recovery and watch his behavior, and speak about his feelings and relationships.

A couple of women got married next to our house, and they are very nice. My kids are asking, "How are they sinners?"

Here, again, what is your reference? Who is the ultimate judge? How can we decide whether this is a sin or not? And by the way, we do not call anyone a sinner, because we are all sinners, but we judge the sin itself. We judge the behavior itself, so this behavior is sinful, and we need to differentiate between morality and spirituality. Some people are very nice and very kind, and you enjoy talking with them. And they are humanitarian, love to help others, and love to serve others. But morality will not get you to heaven. What will get you to heaven is spirituality. Spirituality is your relationship with God. Every spiritual person, a real spiritual person, should be a moral person, but the opposite is not true. Not every moral person is a spiritual person. So yes, there are homosexual people who are very kind, very nice, and very good. But this does not make homosexuality right.

Many youths believe that we should not overreact and make this issue a big deal, and instead, we should show tolerance. How can we address this and explain that this should not be the societal norm, yet still we love those who are homosexual or transgender?

During the voting for legalizing same-sex marriage, many youths, and some of them are Sunday school servants, said to me, "We know it is a sin, but why should I stop somebody from getting married according to their beliefs. This is as if I am restricting their freedom. If they want to choose to live this way, we need to allow them to live this way." And they told me, "Yes, we will vote for same-sex marriage although we do not believe in it." Of course, any belief like this is based on a wrong hypothesis. The definition of freedom here is wrong because freedom without boundaries will hurt the world. As Pope Shenouda said, in his book about freedom, *Ten Concepts*, that the river has two banks. If there are no banks, then the water of the river will turn into a flood. In the same way, freedom should have boundaries. If there are no boundaries for freedom, it will destroy the whole world. They forget that this freedom or this legalization eventually will have an effect on our children and the next generation. I am not just allowing them to get married and live their life as they choose, but I am also hurting my children and grandchildren by approving and agreeing to legalize something sinful.

To answer the question that we are overreacting, we can ask them, "What was the right reaction to COVID?" We saw many people dying, cases were on the rise, and many who survived COVID are left with permanent health problems, so the whole world reacted to this. When the whole world reacted to COVID, churches were even closed during Holy Week and the Feast of Resurrection. Does this mean they hated the people or protected them? The hatred was directed toward the virus, but the protection was for the people out of love. In the same way, homosexuals and transgender people are dying physically, spiritually, psychologically, and emotionally. Others are suffering and are miserable, the cases are growing, and the spread is fast. It is like COVID. The country, the media, the schools, everything around us supports this destructive sin. Then, are you asking why we are reacting? We are reacting to protect the people from this destructive sin. Because people are dying physically, spiritually, emotionally, and psychologically.

God and the Church love homosexuals, and that is why God wants them to live a better and abundant life. They are not living the abundant life. Jesus, when He came, said, "I have come that they may have life, and that they may have it more abundantly."[56] They are not living this better life. This is not hatred; this is love. Hatred is directed toward the sin of homosexuality, not the people. That is why we must react; it is not an overreaction. We need to protect the people from this destructive sin.

---

56   John 10:10.

I have a former Sunday school student who has identified as transgender and is already living that lifestyle publicly. What is my obligation to pursue them or reach out to them?

To respond to this, it is an obligation of love. They are your spiritual son or daughter or student. Again, we need to pray for them, establish a bond of love and care, check on them, and follow up on them. Motivate them, correct the wrong beliefs, establish with them a strong spiritual life, and follow the guidelines of recovery: connecting with oneself, quitting, and connecting with others. And ask the guidance of godly Christian therapists or counselors on how to deal with this person.

How can I handle the topic of homosexuality and transgenderism with toddlers and elementary children? What are some main points I can teach them to be aware of in school?

Being proactive, working with their family, the importance of sexual education and the life of purity, a strong spiritual life, and establishing with them the sources of truth. Again, what is your authoritative reference?

How can I address the subject of transgenderism to a Junior High class?

The children in this age are usually quite argumentative. First, transgenderism includes a wide variety of identities or behaviors. They call it gender dysphoria or gender confusion, or gender identity disorder. It is tough enough for adults to understand this subject, so when our children in middle school or high school encounter this issue, what do we say? And most importantly, how do we help them develop a Biblical, Christian perspective on this issue?

Keep it Simple. We need to keep it simple. Do not get defensive in answering these questions, but just relax and let the Holy Spirit speak through your mouth. Ask for wisdom from God. And as a servant, you are the authority in your students' lives, but you do not have to be an expert on every issue, including this issue of homosexuality and transgenderism. Even the experts do not understand all the complexities of these issues. Do not think you have to understand everything about transgenderism and tell your children everything you know. For example, if they ask you about the gay gene or the gender marks on the brain cell, and you have not read about it or do not know about it, there is nothing wrong with saying that you will look into it and give them an answer. And you can communicate simple truths to them, as I told you before. God made humans male and female. Individuals are born either male or female. Some people get hurt and confused, and they do not like the way God made them. As a result, some people wish to be the other gender or the opposite sex, but nobody can really change from one sex to another. It is medically impossible. And we should not align the body to the mind, but we should align the mind to the body. And keep a dialogue with them. It is not only one session where you answer them, and that is it.

Keep it a Dialogue. When children ask these questions, use this occasion to connect with them; it is a good opportunity to connect with them. "Oh, I like this question. This question will open a dialogue between you and me, and we need to meet several times to completely understand this complex issue." So find out what they are learning, where they learned it from, and what they are thinking. Ask a question like, "Where did you see that? Where did you hear this word? Transgender, for example. Why do you think God made both boys and girls? What do you think transgender means? Do you think a boy can really turn into a girl?" This is an opportunity to get to know your child better. So keep the tone of the conversation friendly. It is not an inquisition but an opportunity to connect with your child. Older children and teens may have more questions, so you might also want to read more from some additional resources; then read and discuss with them in another meeting.

Keep it Truthful. Keep your communication with them truthful. If you do not know the answer to a child's question, say so. There is nothing wrong with saying that you do not know. Then tell your child, "I will look for an answer." Let us say your son asked you, "Why does he want to be a lady?" And the real answer, if we are honest, is, "I don't know why this person wants to be a lady." None of us knows all the pain and the false beliefs in the lives and hearts of homosexuals or transgender people. But Scripture is clear about certain things, and those truths are what you can and should communicate to your children. Again, God made us in His image, male and female. Sin entered the world and spoiled everything, including how we see ourselves. Some people get really hurt and confused as they grow up, but God loves us and sent His Son to save us. God can bring healing and truth to those who are hurt. God wants us to live in the truth about how He created us and who we are. We know God is powerful to save and transform lives, including the gender-confused. Tell your children these truths about God and the people.

Keep it Kind. What do I mean by "keep it kind"? God has a deep love for sexually- and relationally-broken men and women. Yes, believe me, God loves homosexuals and transgender people, including those who are struggling with gender identity issues. These struggles are complicated and tough, and are on deep aspects of our sexuality and being. So the topic can provoke some to laughter or mockery; maybe people have made fun of them or belittled them, or demeaned them. So work to maintain God's heart for the gender confused. As God loves them, we need to love them. God loves them with an everlasting love just as He loves us.[57]

Your children will be watching you for cues about how to respond to gender confusion in individuals and our culture. Pray that God will touch your heart and

---

57   See Jeremiah 31:3.

give you the ability to convey this to your children: you love the transgender, you love the homosexual, although you hate the sin. And the tone and attitude are as important as your words. Share these truths with the children: God loves all of us. God loves men who wish to be women, and God loves women who think they are men, although God hates the sin. You may disagree with one's beliefs and choices; however, you can still be kind and loving to them. We can pray for those who are gender confused so that God can heal them.

Keep it Affirming. What do I mean by "keep it affirming"? When your children see a transgender person, on the news, for example, or on the street, they may feel curious, alarmed, confused, or afraid. So when they ask a question about it, they are not only asking for details about transgenderism, and they are not looking for a lecture on transgenderism, but they are also asking for comfort and affirmation. So, as a servant, you can respond positively. For example, you can say, "I am so glad that God made you a girl and made me also a female." You can ask him or her, "What is good about being a girl, what is good about being a boy?" So you can affirm them in their gender. You can ask the Lord for wisdom and creativity for how to best affirm your sons and daughters in their masculinity and femininity. There are many Christian resources that can give more ideas on talking with your children and helping them grow into strong and secure men and women.

How to equip our children to respond to non-Christians about this topic?

If we do not agree on the source of the truth, then the discussion will be a foolish one. So if the other person is not Christian and does not believe in the authority of the Bible, any discussion will be a foolish discussion. Demand respect for your belief system and your integrity as you show respect to their belief system. And showing respect does not mean agreeing. And if you can challenge the other person to search for the truth, do this in a positive way. Challenge the other person to search for the truth.

What are the signs we should consider as red flags for same-sex attraction?

The first thing is that you cannot figure out or discover these signs or red flags unless you have a good relationship and good communication with your children and your youth. So, for example, if a boy is interested in dolls; the way he dresses; he prefers the company of girls rather than boys especially between the ages of 5 and 12; he prefers the company of older women rather than older men; he is regarded by other boys as feminine, so his classmates regard him as feminine; you find certain gay dating apps on their phones. All these are just red flags of whether or not my son or daughter is suffering or has early signs of homosexuality.